MILLER'S
FIELD GUIDE
SILVER

MILLER'S

Miller's Field Guide: Silver

Miller's, a division of Mitchell Beazley,
both imprints of Octopus Publishing Group Ltd
Endeavour House
189 Shaftesbury Avenue
London
WC2H 8JY
www.octopusbooks.co.uk
Miller's is a registered trademark of Octopus Publishing Group Ltd.

Series Editor:	Judith Miller
Publisher:	Alison Starling
Chief Contributor:	Judith Miller
Editorial Co-ordinator:	Christina Webb
Proofreader:	Jo Murray
Indexer:	Hilary Bird
Art Director:	Jonathan Christie
Designer:	Ali Scrivens, T J Graphics
Production Controller:	Lucy Carter

Copyright © Octopus Publishing Group Ltd 2015
Some of the text in this edition was originally published in *Miller's Antiques Checklist: Silver & Plate* in 1994, reprinted 1995, 1997, 2001.

ISBN 9781784720360

The publishers will be grateful for any information that will assist them in keeping further editions up to date. Although all reasonable care has been taken in the preparation of this book, neither the publishers nor the compilers accept any liability for any consequences arising from the use thereof, nor the information contained herein.

A CIP catalogue record for this book is available from the British Library

Set in Chronicle Deck, Roman, Semibold Italic and Bold
Printed and bound in China

Front cover: A William and Mary tankard, maker 'H.I.' of London.
1693, 8in (20.5cm) high, 30oz, E
Back cover: A Victorian chamberstick, by Francis Higgins of London.
1846, 5in (12.5cm) wide, 4oz, G
Title page: A vegetable dish and cover, by Paul Storr of London.
1806, 9.75in (25cm) diam, 50.5oz, E

A pair of candlesticks, by John Cafe of London. 1755,
9in (23cm) high, 35.5oz, E

Contents

VALUE CODES

Throughout this book the value codes used at the end of each caption correspond to the approximate value of the item. These are broad price ranges and should only be seen as a guide, as prices for antiques vary depending on the condition of the item, geographical location and market trends. The codes used are as follows:

A+++ £150,000+ ($235,000)
A++   £100,000–150,000
      ($165,000-235,000)
A+   £50,000–100,000
      ($80,000-165,000)

A   £25,000–50,000
    ($37,500-80,000)
B   £15,000–25,000
    ($22,000-37,500)
C   £10,000–15,000
    ($15,000-22,000)
D   £5,000–10,000
    ($7,500-15,000)
E   £2,000–5,000 ($3,000-7,500)
F   £1,000–2,000 ($1,500-3,000)
G   £500–1,000 ($750-1,500)
H   £250–500 ($400-750)
J   under £250 (under $400)

Introduction

In Great Britain domestic silver has survived in great quantities from the late 17thC onwards. Ready supplies of the metal coupled with skilled craftsmen and wealthy purchasers combined to produce a legacy that has managed to survive the ravages of war and civil strife virtually unscathed.

English silver has from very early times been stamped with official marks guaranteeing the purity of the metal, and as a by-product this system has provided a record of the date, place of origin and the maker. Originally, a piece was made by the person whose maker's mark was struck on the object, but by the third quarter of the 18thC, when workshop production became popular, this was no longer the case. Frequently, other silversmiths in the factory would make the objects which would then be stamped with the name of the maker whose workshop it was.

In the United States the earliest piece of silver dates to c1651, and any silver from before the middle of the 18thC is very rare. It was not really until the 19thC that the Americans developed

An Elizabeth I Apostle spoon, of St. John, maker's mark unidentified, London. 1562, 6.75in (17cm) long, 1.75oz, C

their own highly decorative style which is collectable today. In the United States there was never a central marking system, and most silver is only stamped with the name or initials of the silversmith, making it difficult to date pieces accurately. Most silver enthusiasts collect silver according to a style that appeals to them. This can be anything from the very plain pieces made at the beginning of the 18thC, to Rococo examples produced 50 years later, and Neo-classical pieces later on in the century. Increasing wealth and new mass-production techniques in the 19thC made silver more readily available, and as a result a greater range of objects and a broader range of quality ensued. However, 19thC silver was held in little esteem until the combined efforts of some leading auction houses and a number of dealers brought it the attention it deserved from buyers. At the upper end of the market is the output of Rundell, Bridge & Rundell, who produced excellent-quality pieces, including many display items; at the other extreme is the variety of inexpensive small wares made to suit new fashions and lower incomes. Highly collectable are Art Nouveau and Art Deco items, as well as pieces that were made by craftsmen such as Gilbert Marks and Omar Ramsden.

If buying at auction, always ask for a condition report. Make sure prices are realistic. The value of a piece of silver depends on a good surface colour, original condition and a lack of repair. If buying at auction, do not go above your set price limit.

When you start a collection, be aware of what you have got. Keep useful records such as catalogues and invoices. Photograph pieces or make a video recording, and keep insurance lists and prices up to date. Having to deal with an insurer with inadequate descriptions is frustrating and you owe it to yourself to look after your property to the best of your ability.

A Liberty & Co. 'Cymric' tea canister and cover, designed by Archibald Knox, Birmingham. 1905, 4in (10cm) high, D

Hallmarks

English hallmarks

The Goldsmiths' Hall in London still strikes silver with hallmarks today. Most English silver has four marks, which, historically, guaranteed that a piece of silver was of the required legal standard.

Although hallmarks are a good guide to age and authenticity they should not be regarded as definitive. This is because they can be worn to illegibility, faked or even let-in from other pieces of metal.

Sterling silver

Sterling is the British term for silver that is at least 92.5% pure. From 1300 the mark was a leopard's head; by 1478 it had a crown. In 1544 it was a

lion passant walking to the left and from 1820 the lion was uncrowned.

Britannia standard

This was a higher standard of silver required between 1697 and 1720. On this silver the town and sterling marks were replaced by Britannia and a lion's head in profile.

The original sterling marks were revived in 1720, but the Britannia mark was sometimes used after that date in order to indicate silver of the higher quality.

The initials used by makers with the Britannia standard are the first two letters of the surname; with sterling silver it is the initials of the Christian name and surname.

Town mark

The mark would vary according to the assay office of the individual town. Sometimes the London mark of a leopard's head was used on provincial silver in addition to the town mark.

Mark for William Ferguson of Peterhead, with Edinburgh marks for 1826

Date letter

The date letter appeared in London from 1478 and later in other parts of the country.

It is unique from year to year as well as assay office to office, but usually follows an alphabetical sequence. The letter is always enclosed by a shield.

Mark for Tiffany & Co.

Marks for Archibald Knox for Liberty & Co., London, 1902.

Maker's mark

Used on silver from 1363, the early marks were signs or symbols, as few people could read; this remained the case until the late 17thC when initials and symbols were combined, the symbols falling from use during the next 100 years.

Sovereign's hand

Used between 1784 and 1890 (and in Dublin from 1807) to indicate that duty had been paid on the item. The mark for George III after 1785 is hard to distinguish from those used for George IV and William IV.

American marks

In the early United States, no national assaying system was adopted, although Baltimore had an assay office between 1814 and 1830. Prior to the adoption of sterling silver as the standard of purity in 1868, silver was obtained from the melting of coins. These could vary in purity, from around .750 millesimal fineness to around .900; therefore, 'coin silver' purity varies. After the sterling standard, pieces were marked with 'STERLING' or with '925'.

Decoration

Surfaces of silver are rarely plain (the exceptions being early 18thC English silver and much 18thC American silver). The main types of decoration are:

Engraving

This involves cutting out a pattern in the silver with a sharp tool. For arms, inscriptions and other marks of ownership, the work was done by hand. The decoration cannot be seen on the reverse. Fine engraving was carried out in Europe, particularly in the Netherlands and Germany. Some of the finest British engravers were William Hogarth, Simon Gribelin and James Sympson. American engraving is rare, but some good examples were produced by Nathaniel Hurd and Joseph Leddel. Unlike British engravers, many American engravers would have signed their work.

Bright-cutting

This was popular at the end of the 18thC. It employs the same methods as engraving, but uses a burnished steel tool to cut the metal. This then polishes the silver as it cuts, producing a sharp design that reflects the light.

Chasing

Chasing appears on silver in the middle of the 17thC and again in the middle of the 18thC. It is a form of relief decoration where the metal is pushed into the required pattern with a hammer or punch, and unlike engraving no silver is removed. The pattern is raised clearly above the surface and the imprint can be seen on the reverse. Common motifs include flowers, foliage and scrolls of various types.

Victorians often decorated earlier silver with chasing. High-quality

A George IV salver, by Rebecca Emes & Edward Barnard I of London. 1825, 10.25in (26cm) diam, 21.5oz, G

chasing was produced by Paul de Lamerie and Amyé Videau in the 18thC. It is sometimes difficult to differentiate between 18thC and 19thC chasing, but genuine 18thC work tends to be more natural and lively compared to the slightly mechanical feel of Victorian work. Silver chasing in the 18thC was marked after it was decorated. When chasing has been added at a later date it will go through the marks – chasing that has been applied first will have the marks superimposed over it.

Chinoiserie

Chinoiserie flat chasing, popular in the late 17thC, incorporates scenes of oriental figures, birds and exotic landscapes into the design. The charmingly naïve subjects are generally very similar and it has been suggested that a single specialist workshop was responsible for all the pieces. Any items of silver chased with chinoiserie decoration are highly collectable and command exceptionally high prices.

Flat chasing

This is the same as chasing, but the decoration appears in low relief. It can be distinguished from engraving as it bears the reverse pattern on the inside.

Cut-card decoration

Good-quality late 17thC and early 18thC pieces of silver are sometimes overlaid with cut-card decoration – pieces of silver, usually in the form of foliage, which are made separately and then soldered to the body to provide attractive reinforcement for the handle sockets or spouts of coffee pots and similar items.

A chinoiserie porringer, maker's mark of 'IY', London. 1690, 5in (12.5cm) high, 9oz, D

Sometimes cut-card decoration is applied beneath the central foot of a piece of silver, in which case it will not be visible. Such decoration is a true sign of quality.

Borders

Border styles can provide some indication to the date that a piece of silver was made. However, it is important to realize that many 18thC borders were repeated in the 19thC.

Gadroon borders were popular on early silver from c1690 to 1700.

On many late 17thC pieces of silver these borders were stamped. They are therefore fragile and, as a result, prone to splitting.

The moulded border was replaced by a simple shell and scroll border in the 1730s.

By the end of the 18thC borders had become plainer. Those dating from 1780 were beaded.

A tankard, by John Seatoune of Edinburgh. 1702, 7.75in (19.5cm) high, 35.5oz, C

Borders from the 1790s and 1800 are either reeded or threaded. By the time of the Regency period borders had become very fancy and elaborate. Cartouches around coats of arms are often similarly intricate and decorative.

Coats of arms

It has always been fashionable for families to engrave their coat of arms, crest or monogram within a decorative cartouche in a prominent place on a piece of silver, especially on larger items. The type of shield and style of cartouche can provide help in dating a piece that lacks a full set of marks, and sometimes it is even possible to trace the arms to a particular individual.

On some large pieces a full set of armorials can appear.

Smaller pieces of silver are usually engraved with crests rather than coats of arms. The difference between a crest and a coat of arms is that a crest may be shared by up to 20 families whereas a coat of arms is traceable to one particular family, or even a man and wife.

Crests are sometimes accompanied by a motto. On English examples the motto is below the crest, on Scottish examples it is above.

Quartering

A son can only quarter the arms of his parents if his mother did not have any brothers. Otherwise, he just uses his father's arms.

Transposed marks

These are sets of marks taken from damaged or low-value objects.

A salver, by James Kerr of Edinburgh, assay master Edward Lothian. 1743, 8.75in (22cm) diam, 14oz, F

Initials

Some early silver is engraved with three initials within a triangle. The upper initial usually represents the family surname, and the lower two are the initials of the first names of the man and wife. Such pieces were often given as wedding presents.

Replacement and erasure of arms

When silver changed hands, the new owners sometimes erased the existing coat of arms and replaced it with their own. This leaves the metal thin and reduces the value, sometimes considerably. If the silver is too thin to be re-engraved, a new coat of arms is sometimes engraved onto the opposite side. Some arms are removed and not replaced.

To see if a coat of arms has been removed you can push with the thumbs on the suspected areas to see if it dents.

Sometimes new arms have been added to an earlier cartouche. These can be identified by the sharper feel of the engraving.

If a new cartouche has been let in to an existing piece of silver the solder line will appear if one breathes on the suspect area.

An Irish teapot and stand, by John Lloyd of Dublin. 1778, stand 5.5in (14cm) diam, 21oz, F

Lighting

Early candlesticks are rare and hardly any appear on the market from before the Restoration of the Monarchy in 1660. Many candlesticks were melted down for coin during the Civil War and this resulted in a physical shortage of silver in the late 17thC. As a result, any candlesticks from this period are disproportionately light because they were hammered up from sheet metal.

By the end of the 17thC candlesticks were cast, and this method of production, which was expensive in both technique and resources, was used until the 1770s when developments in mechanization brought about loaded examples stamped out from sheet.

Cast candlesticks continued to be made in London on a reduced scale after this date, but very rarely in the provinces. Cast candlesticks are stronger than ones hammered from sheet. They tend to be more desirable than loaded ones and command higher prices.

Nozzles are detachable and stop the wax pouring down the stem of the candlestick. They became a regular feature in the 1740s, usually

A pair of Austrian Biedermeier candlesticks, by Mayerhofer & Klinkosch of Vienna. 1850, 10in (25.5cm) high, 23oz, E

conforming in outline to the base and with the same decoration.

Later 17thC candlesticks have fluted columns. However, although candlesticks got progressively taller, there are few variations from the taper or baluster stem apart from a number of mid-18thC Rococo flights of fancy with figural stems, some of which were in the form of a harlequin. As far as American production of candlesticks is concerned very few pairs of candlesticks have survived from the 18thC and early 19thC. This is surprising considering the financial success and high standard of living enjoyed by those living on the Eastern seaboard, along with the obvious need for candle lighting until other methods were discovered.

Candelabra were generally made in the same form as candlesticks. Examples from the beginning of the 18thC are rare and most date from the last quarter of the century onwards. In order to make candelabra more affordable, a number were made with Sheffield plate branches, and these are still less expensive to buy today and provide a more affordable alternative to all-silver examples. Chambersticks from the early 18thC have survived in large numbers. The earlier ones, which are rare today, have the best practical features – a broad handle to give a good grip and a wide platform to catch the drips as the bearer went up to bed. Travelling chambersticks were also made, but like the cased individual

A set of candelabra, by William Pitts & Joseph Preedy of London. 1794, 22in (56cm) high, branches 178oz, A

beakers which came with spice containers and a knife, fork and spoon, these are rare despite their usefulness. A number were still being made at the end of the last century. Candles with self-consuming wicks were not introduced until the 19thC, so up until this time snuffers and their stands were essential. It is again surprising how few have survived compared to the huge numbers that would have been made – after all, every household with silver candlesticks would have had a need for silver snuffers. Most date from the 18thC onwards. Early examples have a simple scissor action, but from the middle of the 18thC various ingenious arrangements were made in an attempt to keep the severed wick in the box. Snuffers were made by specialists, so that although they were made with stands, trays or to fit in the slotted sconces of chamber-sticks, the makers of the snuffers are almost invariably different to that of the tray. Small snuffer trays are usually decorative and well made, and are often sought after in their own right (see pp56–9).

With all candlesticks, candelabra, chambersticks and snuffers, quality and relative weight are important, whether you prefer the plain early

A set of American reeded baluster candlesticks, Tiffany & Co., loaded. 1912–13, 9.75in (25cm) high, D

18thC styles or the exuberance of George IV and later examples. Remember that loaded candlesticks are artificially heavy, and avoid any items in poor condition. A number of cast candlesticks have been faked by simply taking another casting, reproducing everything including the marks; any pair of candlesticks with marks in precisely the same place on each stick is very suspect. Right from the very start of production, candlesticks were made in pairs or sets and despite the passage of time very few appear singly. If they do, there is a substantial reduction in value compared to the price paid for multiples. A genuine pair must be made by the same maker at the same date.

Loaded candlesticks

Mechanization developed during the Industrial Revolution resulted in a proliferation of machine-made loaded candlesticks made in huge numbers to meet the growing

A pair of Liberty & Co. 'Cymric' candlesticks, by Archibald Knox, Birmingham. 1905, 8.5in (21.5cm) high, D

demands of the newly affluent merchant classes. The amount of metal used to make a loaded candlestick was far less than for a cast one, so later candlesticks were significantly lower in price when made, and are still not as desirable.

Candlesticks before 1750

*A pair of candlesticks, by Paul de Lamerie of London.
1737–8, 7.75in (19.5cm) high, 44oz, A+*

1. Is the form relatively simple and robust?
2. Are decorative elements fairly simple, perhaps including rope or circular borders or shell motifs?
3. Do the casting marks line up at the seams? (If not, it could indicate that the piece has been taken apart.)
4. Does it have a detachable nozzle? (If so, it was made from the 1740s onwards.)
5. Are any borders or facets worn or rounded?
6. Is it fully marked under the base or at the foot of the column?
7. Are there, in addition, marks on the sconce and also on the nozzle?
8. Does it measure between 6in (15.5cm) and 10in (25.5cm)?
9. When lifted up does it feel relatively heavy?

Early candlesticks

The earliest English silver table candlesticks date back from before the first half of the 17thC, during the reign of Charles I (1625 –49), though these are very rare.

Any American candlesticks of this period will also be very rare.

A pair of cast candlesticks, by John Le Sage of London. 1725, 7in (18cm) high, 33oz, D

Condition

Throughout the 17thC and first half of the 18thC candlesticks fulfilled a functional rather than decorative role. They were made in vast numbers in simple practical shapes and were used daily. Most survive in pairs rather than singly.

Because of the regular usage to which most were subjected it is not surprising that candlesticks are often in poor condition. In many

cases, well-worn candlesticks were melted down and refashioned, which is another reason for the scarcity of early examples.

Typical characteristics

Throughout the 18thC candlesticks became progressively taller. The one in the main picture measures 7.75in (19.5cm), a typical size for a mid-18thC piece.

Candlesticks made early in the century will usually measure about 6in (15.5cm), and by the end of the century they had doubled in size to about 12in (30.5cm).

Beware

The metal rod with which a loaded candlestick is weighted is held in place by pitch or plaster of Paris. Sometimes this substance will begin to disintegrate inside the silver skin, in which case the piece will rattle if it is gently shaken.

A pair of cast candlesticks, London mark. 1695–1700, 5.25in (13cm) high, 22.25oz, C

Candlesticks 1750–1800

A pair of candlesticks, by John Quantock of London. 1752, 9.25in (23.5cm) high, 41oz, E

1. Is the candlestick cast or loaded?
2. Can the correct marks be seen on the base and nozzle?
3. Are there any holes on the base and column, caused by stretching on areas of high-relief decoration? (This reduces value considerably.)
4. Is there any damage to the leafage?
5. Does the height seem correct for the date of the piece?
6. Is any loading intact?
7. Does the candlestick rattle when shaken? (If so, the loading is loose in the column.)

Mid-18thC candlesticks

By the mid-18thC most candlesticks had detachable nozzles to prevent the molten wax dripping down the sides of the stick.

The shell corners on the base of the candlestick in the main picture were a popular decorative motif of the period.

Repairs

A slightly bent cast candlestick can easily be repaired by a silversmith but this is not true if the stick is loaded as the internal pitch is plaster of Paris and the iron rod would have to be removed before any repairs can take place. Afterwards everything

Two Dutch candlesticks, by Reynert Ringalda of Amsterdam. 1775 and 1769, 9.5in (24cm) high, 32.75oz, D

has to be put back and this is time consuming and expensive. The same is true for sticks with defective loading. The metal on a loaded stick is also fairly thin and this makes any solder repairs more difficult.

A popular innovation that was introduced at the turn of the 19thC was the telescopically extending candlestick. These were chiefly produced in Sheffield, and always made by using the loaded technique. Large numbers of plate telescopic candlesticks were also made. Telescopically extending candlesticks were only made for about ten years.

A pair of Masonic candlesticks, by Frederick Vonham of London. 1759, 13.5in (34cm) high, E

Candlesticks 1750-1800

A pair of French candlesticks, maker's mark 'AL', Paris, with ovolo and tied reeded foot rims and cast octagonal baluster stems with shells. 1748, 8in (20.5cm) high, 34.5oz, B

A pair of George II candlesticks, by John Quantock of London, with typical shell capitals and knopped stems, with shell motifs. 1757, 9in (23cm) high, 34oz, E

A pair of Rococo-style Augsburg candlesticks, by Johann Balthasar Hechenauer. The spiral fluting on the baluster-shaped shaft gives the characteristic assymetrical appearance. 1761, 8.25in (21cm) high, 19.5oz, D

A pair of George III loaded candlesticks, by John Carter II of London, each raised from a moulded hexafoil base with anthemion angles below a knopped fluted stem. 1768, 10.25in (26cm) high, F

A pair of George III cast silver table candlesticks, by William Cafe of London, with traditional knopped stem raised on serpentine square bases. 1774, 7.75in (19.5cm) high, E

A pair of George III candlesticks, by John Cafe of London, of scrolling Rococo style with acanthus leaf detail. 1788, 9.75in (25cm) high, E

A set of three George III candlesticks, by George Ashworth & Co. of Sheffield, the fluted oval bases rising to flared stems supporting vase-shaped nozzles, with reeded borders. 1797, 12in (30.5cm) high, E

A pair of Flemish Neo-classical candlesticks, bearing a monogram, maker's mark 'LB', hallmark Lüttich. 1798-1809, 10in (25.5cm) high, 27oz, E

19thC candlesticks

A set of four candlesticks, by
Paul Storr of London. 1811–12, 9in
(23cm) high, 118oz, A++

1. Are the candlesticks in a revival style?
2. Are they larger in size than the originals?
3. Is the overall decoration elaborate?
4. Can the correct marks be seen on the base and nozzle?
5. Is there any damage to the leafage?
6. Do they employ figural subjects?

19thC candlesticks

By the middle years of the 19thC silversmiths looked increasingly to the past for their inspiration. By the end of the century manufacturers were eagerly copying any previous style from the 18thC that they thought suitable, in both larger and smaller versions than the originals. The styles were also applied to the manufacture of candelabra. Few cast candlesticks were made during

A pair of French Louis XVI-style candlesticks, by Andrew Debain. c1900, 13in (33cm) high, E

A pair of Rococo Revival candlesticks, by Waterhouse, Hodson & Co. of Sheffield. 1829, 10.5in (26.5cm) high, E

the later 19thC because the process became prohibitively expensive compared with the new mechanized manufacturing techniques. Surface decoration became increasingly important and elaborate throughout this period, in keeping with the Victorian love of covering plain surfaces with excessive decoration. Stamping is vulnerable to damage caused by the stretching of the silver sheet, so candlesticks made using this technique should always be carefully checked for holes in the decoration as they will lower the value.

Figural subjects

By the end of the 19thC many candlesticks were adorned with figures, such as putti, cherubs or shepherds and shepherdesses. They typically have the putti holding aloft a *torchère* issuing a foliate-cast nozzle, with all-over foliate scrolls.

Authenticity

If there are any signs of wear on the decoration, the gilding could have been applied at a later date and this is less desirable.

Early 20thC candlesticks

A pair of Kalo candlesticks. c1925, 14in (35.5cm) high, C

1. Is the candlestick in the fashionable Arts and Crafts or Art Nouveau style?
2. Is it fully marked?
3. Is it in the Rococo Revival style?
4. Is it simply decorated with a hammered surface?
5. Is the central figure a *'femme-fleur'*?

Figural candlesticks

As the predominant styles of the period were the curvaceous Art Nouveau and the much more austere Arts and Crafts, both were reflected in the style of candlesticks made. The Arts and Crafts style is apparent in the Kalo sticks opposite and the Art Nouveau by the sticks by Williams of Birmingham. Arts and Crafts decoration could also include medieval, romantic and folk art. The Rococo Revival was still a dominant style, particularly in areas such as Russia and France.

The workshop of Williams of Birmingham was renowned for

A pair of candlesticks, by Williams of Birmingham. c1906, 11in (28cm) high, D

its production of good-quality, decorative pieces of silver at the end of the Victorian period. This pair of figural candlestick are in the fashionable Art Nouveau style. Figural candlesticks continued to be produced throughout the 19thC and beyond. Among other variations which appear on the market are:

• similar figures, but in the form of two-light candelabra.

• other rustic subjects such as shepherds and gardeners.

• pairs often represent a male and female figure, rather than two identical ones.

A pair of Fabergé Rococo-style candlesticks, workmaster Julius Rappoport of St Petersburg. 1908–17, 6in (15.5cm) high, 36oz, B

27

Chambersticks

A pair of chambersticks, by John Schofield of London.
1780, 5.25in (13cm) diam, 18oz, F

1. Is the pan marked in a line under the base?
2. Are the detachable parts (the extinguisher and nozzle) marked with the same marks?
3. Does the border on the pan and nozzle match?
4. Have there been any repairs made to the feet or handles?
5. Is there any sign of a crest having been removed from the pan or extinguisher?

Chambersticks

Chambersticks were made to hold a candle to light the way to bed and consequently they have been made in considerable numbers. Early examples from the end of the 17thC

A small chamberstick, by Yapp & Woodward of Birmingham. 1848, 3.75in (9.5cm) diam, 2.25oz, G

have flat handles, but these are exceptionally rare as probably not many were made at this time; most chambersticks date from the second half of the 18thC and disappear as soon as gas lighting was introduced in the late 19thC. Some of them must have been made in sets as all members of a family would need one. Plated examples were often made and these are usually very elaborate, with some having a glass shade to protect the flame against the wind; these shades would not often survive. Because chambersticks have been used so much they tend not to be in good condition. They are usually sold singly, but any sold in pairs will fetch a premium.

Typical features

Borders on the pans of chambersticks tend to follow those found on corresponding salvers of the time. From c1720 the ring or scroll handle was standard on chambersticks; it would often have a slot to take a conical extinguisher. A slot in the centre is for an extinguisher, probably of the scissor type, but surprisingly, these were made separately and by different makers. It is important that chambersticks are fully marked as inkstands were made with chambersticks attached and sometimes these may be sold separately, in which case they will only be part-marked, although they will of course be smaller.

A chamberstick, by Tiffany & Co. of New York. 1886, 10.5in (26.5cm) long, 7.5oz, G

Candelabra

A pair of candelabra, by Jones & Schofield of London. c1776
16.5in (42cm) high, 69.75oz, A

1. Are all detachable pieces marked? The branches should be fully marked.
2. Do the designs of the sconce, branch and candlestick all match each other?
3. Are the branches intact? (It is virtually impossible to repair broken loaded arms.)
4. If the candlestick is cast is its base loaded? (A common way of adding extra weight needed for stability.)
5. Is there any evidence of cracking below the sconce or at the base of the stem?

Candelabra

Candelabra dating from earlier than the late 18thC are very exceptional. Candelabra follow the same forms and styles as candlesticks. Most were made in pairs and had detachable branches that were cast or loaded, and which fitted into the sconce at the top of the central column. Early ones had two arms, by the end of the 18thC three were usual, and during the 19thC candelabra with up to five or more arms were made. Candelabra were always several times more expensive than candlesticks and were produced in lesser quantities.

Sizes became progressively taller throughout the 18thC, reaching their peak in the Regency period.
During the later part of the 19thC, following the introduction of gas lighting, sizes tended to diminish slightly. On early candelabra the branches could be removed and the

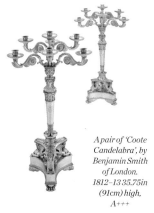

A pair of 'Coote Candelabra', by Benjamin Smith of London. 1812–13 35.75in (91cm) high, A+++

central stem used as a candlestick. On later candelabra this dual usage was impossible because the stem grew too high and the nozzle grew too wide to hold a candle. The decoration of the different parts of the candelabrum should match, indicating that everything belongs together.

A pair of candelabra, by William Pitts & Joseph Preedy of London, loaded. 1790 and 1794, 22in (56cm) high, branches 87oz, B

31

Candelabra

A pair of French seven-light candelabra, by Jean-Baptiste-Claude Odiot of Paris, each with a tapered torchère standard, chased with trailing bell flowers and a wreath cast base. c1830, 27.5in (70cm) high, A

A pair of William IV candelabra, by Edward I, Edward II, John & William Barnard of London, decorated with 'C'- and 'S'-scrolls, flower heads and acanthus leaves. 1831, 22.5in (57cm) high, 320oz, B

A pair of mid-19thC Italian four-light candelabra, by Filippo Pansi, with knopped stem and spiral fluted central section, three scrolling branches. c1840, 18.25in (46.5cm) high, 70oz, E

A pair of late 19thC Rococo Revival candelabra, one by J. C. Klinkosch of Vienna, one by Robert Garrard of London, with elaborate floral decoration and sculpted putti. 29in (73cm) high, 58oz, A

*A pair of German seven-light candelabra,
after Christian Erich Ingermann, one with
maker's mark 'Mau Dresden', with typical
moulded rocailles and grape decoration.
1888, 21in (53cm) high, 277oz, B*

*A pair of late Victorian five-light candelabra,
by Hawksworth, Eyre & Co. Ltd., of Sheffield,
the stems of knopped and tapering form with
leaf detail, the bases with scroll shell detail to
the corners. 1899, 19in (48cm) high, D*

*A three-branch candelabra, by Tiffany &
Co. of New York, decorated with repoussé
flowers and a feather design, the side arms
are curving swan heads decorated with
applied leaves, marked 'Tiffany & Co. 5992
Makers 5989 Sterling Silver 925-1000 M'.
c1900, 17in (43cm) high, 110oz, D*

*A pair of Arts and Crafts candelabra, by
James Dixon & Sons of Sheffield. The
simple lines and hammered decoration are
typical features of the style. 1906, 8.75in
(22cm) high, D*

Dining silver

Silver tableware ranges from rare and expensive soup tureens and sets of plates to everyday necessities like salt cellars. Also covered in this section are snuffers, because although these are not strictly dining silver, they were very necessary pieces in the dining room.

Meat plates are particularly popular with collectors. Large quantities have survived from the beginning of the 18thC because many were made to satisfy the demands of wealthy families. Meat plates command high prices, and because soup plates are used far less often, many of them have been altered into meat plates over the years. As a result soup plates are rare, but despite this they are still less expensive than meat plates. Borders of plates were frequently replaced to keep abreast with contemporary fashions, and any that have been altered should be avoided – remember, technically it is illegal to own them and it is certainly an offence to sell them. When buying plates, those with a shell and gadroon border are popular because they are easy to match and can be made into larger sets. Plates with a plain round gadroon border are not as collectable and are less expensive. Any Queen Anne plates command a premium, even when sold singly.

Shaped oval meat dishes were made *en suite* with round meat plates. Most popular are the very small and the very large. Those dating from the beginning of the 18thC are rare. From the 1750s onwards dishes were occasionally fitted with a mazarine, a pierced insert that effectively gave the dish a base suitable for serving fish from. Mazarines are rare today, but the best examples with attractive piercing and engraving are popular with collectors.

The surface of plates and dishes is always plain and any ornamentation is in the border, with crests or coats of arms usually engraved on the rims. On salvers and trays, however, crests and arms are a prominent central feature and on many of them the engraving is magnificent. The whole surface can also be decorated, either with engraving or flat chasing, depending on the period. Because crests and arms are so important on salvers and trays it is essential to be able to identify them and recognize any later additions as these will lower the value considerably.

Sauce boats are mostly plain apart from a crest or coat of arms, although there are a few very elaborate Rococo examples that stand on rock-like bases and have highly imaginative handles. With the onset of Neo-classicism in the 1770s, sauceboats gave way to sauce and soup tureens, and from this time onwards sauce and soup tureens were often made to match – single sauceboats are far less desirable. Soup tureens are extremely expensive and anyone who can afford to buy one should be particular about condition. A base increases the value of a soup tureen considerably, but examples frequently appear without them. Other large serving items made in silver include entrée dishes. These were made in pairs and are only collectable as such today. It is important that lids have not been mixed up within a large set as this will prevent them from sitting properly on the bases. Large silver dinner services, like the one below, are particularly desirable, especially by a good late 19thC Viennese maker such as Mayerhofer, Klinkosch and Schiffer. The service also has a substantial weight of silver. The crest of Earl Henckel von Donnersmarck is also a sign of quality and that applies

A late 19thC Vienna silver dinner service, by Mayerhofer and Klinkosch and Schiffer, with the crest of Earl Henckel von Donnersmarck. plate 10in (25.5cm) diam, 661oz, B

to any crest denoting someone of nobility. This service contained 19 dinner plates, three large round platters, two large oval platters, and one small and one large tureen. All elements had lobed borders and groove decoration.

At the more affordable end of the dining silver market are snuffer trays and cruet frames. Snuffers were made in high quantities. The earliest type of 18thC snuffer stand resembled a candlestick and held the snuffers upright inside the body. Cruet frames were first made in c1725. Check those with glass bottles as they are prone to damage. Also, the larger types may look impressive, but they are not very usable today.

Individual salt cellars and mustard pots provide two of the most attractive and varied collecting areas in silver, particularly those dating from the Victorian period which were made in a great variety of shapes and sizes. Unfortunately, the greatest enemy of the salt cellar is salt, so be meticulous about

emptying it from the container when not in use. Pepper casters from the early 18thC can be magnificent and cost thousands of pounds, but most of them are relatively simple and affordable. Remember, however, that the piercing is now too large for today's fine pepper. Mustard pots were made singly but casters and salt cellars were made in pairs and any still together fetch a premium. Finally in this section is flatware. Here it is important to find a pattern that appeals personally, and which can be added to or made up in the event of loss. Antique knives with loaded handles are not a practical proposition, particularly those with steel blades as these rust easily and are worth very little; modern equivalents are a far better buy. It is essential to buy flatware in good condition. It should also be heavy, stand up to wear and feel comfortable in the hand. Most expensive to buy are 'straight sets', where each piece has been made at the same date by the same maker, but it is perfectly possible and far cheaper to buy in smaller groups – for example, a set of six spoons and forks. In all cases, the greater variation in the dates and makers, the cheaper the price.

The rather grand late 19thC covered tureen opposite was made by the eminent New York silversmiths, Ball, Black & Co. The stag handles and finial add to its decorative appeal. It would undoubtedly have been one of a pair or a set of four. It has the numerical mark '950' which denotes the purity of the silver.

Due to the wealth of the burgeoning middle classes and merchants in the 19thC, silver from that period is much more readily available today and therefore checking its condition is essential.

The Arts and Crafts salts and spoons below are by the prominent designer Charles Robert Ashbee. The spiral stylized pierced leaf supports are particularly desirable.

A pair of salts and spoons, by Charles Robert Ashbee for the Guild of Handicraft, London. 1900, salts 3in (7.5cm) diam, F

Plates

A rare tazza, by John Yourston of Edinburgh, assay master James Penman. 1698, 9in (23cm) diam, 11.5oz, D

1. Are the plates marked clearly in a line underneath?
2. Have the marks been stretched in any way?
3. Is the date of the hallmark consistent with the style of the border on the plate?
4. Is there a coat of arms or crest? Is it contemporary to the period of the plate?
5. Is there any evidence of a coat of arms or crest having been removed?
6. Are there any scratches or knife marks on the surface? (If not, the plates are worth considerably less as it suggests they have been over-polished.)

Dining plates

The standard dinner service comprised six dozen meat plates and two dozen soup plates, with oval meat dishes made to match in any numbers up to 30 (usually in fours for the smaller sizes, and singles for the larger ones). Dinner plates today tend to be sold in dozens. The largest and smallest sized meat dishes are the most popular. On the other hand,

A set of six plates, by Augustin Le Sage of London. 1776, 9.75in (25cm) diam, 102.75oz, E

soup plates have little use today and consequently they are a lot less expensive, even though they are considerably rarer.

Shapes and styles

With the exception of very early dinner plates (1710–20), shape has altered little, and any changes have been to the borders. Earlier plates had broader borders and often these have been removed and new ones put on to bring them in line with fashion. To do this, the plate had to be reshaped and part of the original flange put into the body. Plates were originally marked underneath in a line very close to the depression with the border and when altered it was impossible not to damage the mark, so any unmarked plates will have been reshaped. Always check marks match the style of the border.

Early plates up until the reign of George I nearly always have a coat of arms; later plates will sometimes have a crest.

Very rarely, plates have an additional royal coat of arms, which indicates that the silver was an official issue. Such items are particularly desirable.

A dinner plate, by John Samuel Hunt of London. 1853, 10.75in (27.5cm) diam, 16.25oz, H

Entrée dishes

A set of 'Rutland Marine Service' silver entrée dishes, covers and liners, by Benjamin Smith II of London. 1807, 12.5in (32cm) long, 523oz, A++

1. Do the cover and base match? (Do they bear corresponding numbers or groups of dots?)
2. Are the cover and base fully marked, and the handles part-marked with the lion passant and duty mark?
3. Is there a coat of arms, or at least a crest, covering quite a large area?
4. Is the metal thin or worn where a coat of arms may have been removed?
5. Does the handle fit properly?
6. On dishes with screw-in handles, is the metal damaged around the socket?
7. If there is a heater base, is the plating in good condition? Is there any bleeding from the lead due to excess heat?
8. Is the heater compartment on the base still intact?

Entrée dishes

Entrée dishes were used for keeping food on a sideboard, or for serving food at a table.

By the 1780s they were always made with lids. Earlier entrée dishes tend to be oval in shape. Later ones are cushion-shaped or rectangular. The lids gradually become more domed from the Regency period onwards. Entrée dishes appear to have died out by the 1830s, at which point they were often circular in shape or reproductions of older styles.

Heater bases

From the beginning of the 19thC many of the entrée dishes came with silver-plated heater bases, which were either filled with hot water or a lump of heated iron.

This George III entrée dish below was made by Paul Storr for Rundell, Bridge & Rundell in 1808 and shows

a progression from earlier borders on the cover of the dish to a collar. Despite the elaborate decoration, there is still space for a decorative coat of arms on the cover. The shape of the body is now cushion-shaped, rather than rectangular, and the top

A pair of vegetable tureens and covers, by William Burwash of London, with Sheffield plate stands. 1815, 10.5in (26.5cm) high, E

is significantly more domed than on earlier examples. The elaborate detachable handle on the dish is typical of Storr's work.

Marks

The dish's base and cover should be fully marked in a straight line and should include the duty mark from 1784 onwards.

Other detachable parts of entrée dishes should all bear the maker's mark along with the lion passant.

An entrée dish and cover, by Paul Storr of London. 1808, 13.5in (34cm) long, 76oz, E

Entrée dishes

A set of four George IV entrée dishes and covers, by Philip Rundell of London, with shell and foliate scroll borders, and lion rampant handles, engraved with a coat of arms and a presentation inscription. 1822, 12in (30.5cm) long, 350oz, A+

A Victorian covered entrée dish, by Paul Storr of London, the base with twin shell-form handles. 1838, 12.75in (32.5cm) wide, E

A Victorian covered entrée dish, by Robert Garrard of London, surmounted by a griffin finial and engraved with a coat of arms. 1854, 11in (28cm) diam, E

One of a pair of 19thC entrée dishes, covers and liners, by Robert Gordon of Calcutta, the pull-off domed covers with fluted section and simple reeded twist handle. 9in (23cm) diam, 66oz, G

A pair of American covered entrée dishes by Tiffany & Co., the lids with handles, the bodies having handled liners, raised on four feet. c1870, 11.in (28cm) wide, 86.25oz, D

A covered entrée dish, by Dominick & Haff of New York, with an all-over foliate and floral repoussé decoration and loop handle. 1886, 11in (28cm) long, 48oz, E

An entrée dish by Ball, Black, & Co. of New York, with a simple shape and a distinctive stag finial. c1900, 12in (30.5cm) diam, 39.7oz, F

A pair of Edwardian entrée dishes and covers, by Walker & Hall of Sheffield, with gadrooned edges and detachable handles. 1902, (11.5in) 29cm long, 132.25oz, E

Sauceboats

A sauceboat, by Robert Gordon of Edinburgh, with dolphin 'S'-scroll handle. 1752-3, 6.75in (17cm) long, 7oz, D

1. Is the form a typical bulbous boat shape?
2. Does it stand on three feet?
3. Has the body been made in one piece (and is it therefore seamless)?
4. Is any decoration on the body confined to a crest or coat of arms?
5. Does the border on the rim both decorate and reinforce the body? (Those with waved edges often have splits in them.)
6. Is the scroll or flying scroll handle securely attached to the body?
7. Are the marks clearly defined?

Sauceboats

Although sauces had been served with food in the 17thC the earliest sauceboats date from the reign of George I (1714–27). The sauceboat opposite is a typical mid-18thC example, with a plain, fairly deep body, three feet and a scroll handle. Decoration is characteristically restrained – confined to a gadrooned border that serves to strengthen the lip, and shells adorning the feet. The development of later styles in sauceboats was largely determined by practical considerations. Silver is an efficient conductor of heat, but this also means that hot contents grow cold quickly, particularly in sauceboats with feet.

Towards the end of mainstream production of sauceboats (c1745–65) central feet returned to favour,

the bowl tended to be deeper and the spout tended to be wider and more raised. Decorative borders became more noticeable.

Later sauceboats

The sauceboat returned to favour after the Regency period and continued to be made throughout

A pair of sauceboats, by William Robertson of Edinburgh. c1755, 8in (20.5cm) long, 24.25oz, F

the Victorian period.

Most 19thC sauceboats were developed in imitation of 18thC styles, although one or two highly elaborate and original Regency pieces were produced.

Damage

The feet on sauceboats are vulnerable to damage and may get bent out or pushed into the body.

Marks

Marks are usually placed in a straight line under the body.

A sauceboat, by William Darker of London. c1726, bowl 4in (10cm) diam, 5.75oz, G

Sauceboats

A pair of George II sauceboats, by William Grundy of London, of oval-bellied form with gadrooned borders and leaf-capped scroll handles resting on shell and scroll feet. 1757, 8in (20.5cm) long, 29oz, E

A George II sauceboat, of plain bombé-sided form, with waved rim and acanthus-capped double scroll handle, on three shell-capped scroll legs and hoof feet, London. 1759, 5in (12.5cm) wide, 4oz, H

A George III sauceboat, by William Skeen of London, on three shell and hoof feet, with leaf-capped flying scroll handle. 1766, 7.5in (19cm) long, F

A George III sauceboat, by John Arnell of London, with a leaf-capped flying scroll handle, a beaded rim and three shell and hoof feet. 1775, 6.75in (17cm) long, 9oz, G

A pair of Irish provincial sauceboats, by Carden Terry of Cork, of bellied shape, with flying scroll handle, bead border, crested, on three feet. c1780, 6.75in (17cm) long, 16.25oz, E

A Victorian sauceboat, by Martin, Hall & Co. of Sheffield, with shaped rims, leaf-capped flying scroll handle, anthemion and trefid feet. 1898, 7.5in (19cm) long, 9oz, G

An Arts and Crafts sauce bowl with attached undertray, by Robert Jarvie of Chicago. The teardrop-shaped bowl with spout, long jutting, hollow, angular square handle is classic Arts and Crafts. c1925, 8.5in (21.5cm) long, E

A 1950s Georg Jensen sauceboat, model no. 896, designed by Jorgen Jensen, with ebonized wood handle, stamped marks. 7in (18cm) wide, G

Sauce tureens

A pair of sauce tureens and covers, by Daniel Smith,
Robert Sharp & Thomas Ellis of London. 1782, 9in
(23cm) long, 44.75oz, F

1. Is the shape elegant and refined?
2. Is the cover marked on a flange with the maker's mark and, possibly, a lion passant and duty mark?
3. Does the lid fit snugly into the base?
4. Do any numbers or dots on the body match those on the lid?
5. Does any crest on the body match those on the lid?
6. If the lid has a finial, is it attached with a screw rather than solder? (A sign of quality.)
7. Has the foot remained in its original position?
8. If there is any decoration, is it relatively restrained?
9. Is there a central pedestal foot, and has it been pushed up into the body?

Sauce tureens

Lidded sauce tureens became popular in the 1770s. The tureens opposite were made in 1782 and show the elegant two-handled shape that is typical of the late 18thC. Sauce tureens continued to be popular until the early 19thC when they were replaced by ceramic ones.

Like sauceboats, sauce tureens were made in pairs or larger sets, often

A pair of sauce tureens, by John Romer of London. c1770, 10in (25.5cm) long, 28oz, F

to match soup tureens. If the sauce tureen has originally been part of an extensive suite it may have an identifying number. If the lid does not fit well it could have become separated from the correct base and the value may be affected.

Decoration

Decoration on Classical-style tureens remained relatively restrained. Some more ornate examples were made with bud finials and applied swags, but these are much rarer and are always expensive.

Less expensive sauce tureens have chased swags; more expensive ones have cast swags and applied decoration and also tend to be heavier pieces.

Condition

Separately applied parts can be particularly vulnerable to damage.

Marks

All separate parts – cover, handle and base – should be marked at least with the maker's mark. A full set of marks should appear on the body.

Collecting

Shapes can affect values. The more elegant forms tend to be most sought after by collectors. Oblong sauce tureens are not generally popular and are the least valuable.

Reproductions

In the late 19thC, heavy and ornate tureens on four feet, which were based on early 17thC designs, became popular once again.

A matched set of sauce tureens and covers, by John Wakelin & Robert Garrard, London. 1800, 9.5in (24cm) long, 89oz, D

Sauce tureens

A pair of George III silver sauce tureen covers, by Paul Storr of London, in a plain oval form, simple but not as commercial as more decorative pieces. They are on later frosted glass tureen bases. 1802, 7.5in (19cm) long, 12oz, F

A pair of George III sauce tureens, by William Bennett of London in a simple rectangular form with gadrooned borders and engraved with an armorial. 1806, 7.5in (19cm) long, 32oz, F

A George III sauce tureen and cover, by Benjamin Smith II of London, with a good foliate scroll handle above leaves to the nulled domed covers, shell and gadrooned rims. 1814, 8.25in (21cm) long, 28oz, F

A set of George III sauce tureens and covers, by Paul Storr of London, applied with trailing oak leaves and acorns, with lion rampant finials, on acanthus leaf and shell scroll bracket feet, with silver liners. 1816, 10.25in (26cm) long, 256oz, A++

A Victorian sauce tureen and cover, by John Waterhouse for Edward Hatfield & Co., Sheffield, with foliate scroll handles, on foliate feet, the cover with shell and scroll rims. 1837, 8.75in (22cm) long, 38oz, E

An oval floral-moulded sauce tureen, by Kirk & Son, New York, with gilt liner and unusual sculpted lion-head finial. c1840, 7.25in (18.5cm) high, 25oz, F

An Edwardian sauce tureen and cover, by Nathan & Hayes of Chester, with reeded loop handle and borders, the cover with Classical urn finial. 1901, 9in (23cm) long, 14oz, H

An early 20thC Belgian lidded tureen, by Leysen Frères of Brussels. The rim with typical leaf-and-dart band, and the cover with a sculpted pineapple. It has the purity mark '950'. 12in (30.5cm) high, 114oz, D

Soup tureens

*A soup tureen and cover, by George Wickes of London,
on four lion-mask and claw-and-ball capped feet.
1737, 18.5in (47cm) long, 129.75oz, A*

1. Is the piece fully hallmarked under the base?
2. Is the cover also fully marked (less the town mark)?
3. Is the coat of arms contemporary, or has an old one been removed?
4. Is there any damage to the body? (Check the body has not sunk
    into the base.)
5. Is there any beaded decoration? (This dates it to either c1780
    or c1860.)
6. Does it have loop handles, pedestal foot and batswing fluting?

Soup tureens

Most soup tureens date from the reign of George III or later; earlier ones do exist, but anything before 1750 is very rare. They were very large and expensive and only relatively grand houses could afford them. They are usually oval, which is the most desirable shape. The handles of soup tureens tend to be more inventive than those of sauce tureens. Early soup tureens were made as singles, but later ones were occasionally made as pairs. Nearly all were made in London. Very elaborate tureens were made in the Rococo period of the 1720s and 1750s using fish and shells as decoration. In the Regency period some tureens were made with Egyptian motifs, others inspired by Napoleon's campaigns.

Liners

Soup tureens with a complicated shape were sometimes made with liners which are frequently made from Sheffield plate rather than from silver.

A soup tureen and cover, by Daniel Smith & Robert Sharp of London. 1783, 18in (46cm) wide, 90oz, D

Marks

The base should be fully marked and lids with the leopard's head, maker's mark and the sovereign's head.

Beware

An elaborate cartouche encircles a crest that is later than the piece, so check the body for thinness where an earlier crest may have been removed.

Bases

Some examples were made with a large, two-handled base to which it would be attached by screws that would go up into the bottom of the feet. If the feet of a tureen have threaded holes the tureen should come accompanied by a base.

A soup tureen and cover, by Paul de Lamerie of London. 1747-8, 14.5in (37cm) wide, 116oz, A+

Soup tureens

A Regency soup tureen and cover, by John Houle of London, the gadrooned rim and leaf-cast handles and lobed body raised on four leaf-cast feet with scrolled toes.
1811, 16in (40.5cm) wide, C

A George III soup tureen and cover, by Paul Storr of London, with a domed lid with a boat finial, the base with ball-cast rim and two similar scrolling handles, on spreading oval foot with ball-cast edge. 1812, 18.5in (47cm) wide, F

A German silver ornamental tureen, with the maker's mark 'Gebrüder Gerike' Scheffler 1739, assayer's mark 'Tremolierstich', Berlin hallmark and mark of B. G. F. Andreak. It has a gilt interior and two sculpted St Mark's lions supporting the tureen, and a sculpted lion finial on the lid, the handles are mythical beasts. c1830, 17in (43cm) high, 233.5oz, B

A serving tureen, by Moore for Tiffany & Co. of New York, NY, the curved handles ending in bifurcate scrolls and flat leaves, the cover with tooled ovolo band, and the body with geometric and beaded rims. 1854-70, 12.5in (32cm) high, 72oz, D

A late 19thC stag-head soup tureen, retailed by Shreve, Stanwood & Co., Boston, MA, with beaded accenting, leaf-tip and beaded rims, with cast stag-head handles, the ring-form handle topped by a hops finial centred by a stag's head. 18.5in (47cm) wide, 85oz, C

A silver tureen and silver liner, by John Edward Bingham of Sheffield, with a band of leaf decoration and an applied Classical head and motto. It stands on hairy-paw feet with Classical pillar legs. 1891, 2.8in (20.5cm) high, 82oz, E

A 20thC Peruvian covered tureen, with a leafy knop and loop handles, raised on claw-and-ball feet. 12.5in (32cm) wide, G

A French Art Deco tureen, cover and stand, by Tetard Frères of Paris. The clean lines and lack of decoration are typical of French metalwork of the 1920s. 14in (35.5cm) long, 182oz, C

Snuffer trays

A pair of candle snips and snuffer stand, by Simon Panton I of London, crested. 1719, stand 7.75in (19.5cm) high, D

1. Are both snuffers and tray of the same date? (The closer together in time they are, the better.)
2. If the snuffers and tray are crested, do the crests match each other?
3. Has a crest been removed from either the tray or snuffers?
4. Does the pair of snuffers still have its tip? (Any damage will reduce value.)
5. Is there any wear to the pivot on the snuffers?
6. Is the tray fully marked under the base with a mark in each corner?
7. Are any snuffers marked on both sides?

Snuffers

Snuffers, of a scissor form, were used for trimming wicks that had not burnt down with the candles. They were made in substantial numbers as it was only in the 19thC that candles consumed their wicks. The earliest snuffers and trays commonly seen date from the beginning of the 1700s. Although they were probably retailed as sets, most snuffers and trays were not made by the same maker. Usually candlestick makers produced the trays, while specialists produced the snuffers. Apart from the early 18thC examples where the stand was made

A snuffer tray, by Gawen Nash of London. 1737, 7.5in (19cm) long, 8oz, G

vertically like a candlestick, few snuffers have their original stands. Designs changed little between the 18thC and 19thC.
Keeping the cut wick in the top proved a problem. The most ingenious solution was to use a blade operating vertically out of line with the cut, which closed off half the box while the wick was trimmed.

Condition

Snuffer trays are collectable in their own right as most were well made and

A snuffer stand, the maker's mark worn, London. 1764, 7in (18cm) wide, 8oz, H

have usually survived in reasonable condition. Except for the candlestick variety, most are relatively inexpensive.
During the 19thC silver was more often replaced by plate for snuffers and such examples are widely available and very affordable. Silver ones are far rarer.
Any crest or arms on snuffers should ideally match those on the tray.

Beware

Pen trays and snuffers' trays are frequently converted into more expensive objects such as inkstands. Conversions, however, will not have matching marks on all the parts.

Snuffer's trays

A snuffer and undertray, by silversmiths 'IB' and 'JG'. It is not unusual to find maker's marks that are still unrecognized. In this instance, it is the quality of the piece that will determine the price. c1766 and c1751, tray 7.75in (19.5cm) wide, 13.5oz, F

An early George III candle snuffer and tray, by Ebenezer Coker of London, with a scroll handle and monogrammed thumbpiece, raised on four swept shell-shaped feet, with foliate engraved decoration. 1763 and 1768, 8in (20.5cm) wide, 13.25oz, H

An 18thC German snuffer tray, maker's mark 'IBH', Augsburg, waisted with scalloped ends and an upswept handle. c1767, 7in (18cm) long, 4.5oz, H

A pair of George III candle snuffers and tray, of Neo-classical design, by Charles Goodwin of London. 1804, tray 9.5in (24cm) wide, G

A candle snuffer by Rebecca Emes &
Edward Barnard I of London, with
ornate acanthus leaf decoration and
internal wick trimmer, is engraved
with a rampant lion. 1808-27, 8in
(20.5cm) long, 7oz, G

A snuffer tray, by John & Thomas
Settle, Gunn & Co., of Sheffield, the
tray is decorated with floral repoussé
on a stipple ground with a lion
rampant in the centre. 1826, 9.7in
(24.6cm) long, 9oz, G

A Portuguese snuffer and tray, by
Joano Pires Esteves of Oporto, the
tray with a shaped pierced gallery and
on four pierced feet. 1853-61, snuffers
5.25in (13cm) long, 6oz, H

A late Victorian cigar cutter, by
H. Matthews of Birmingham,
in the form of a pair of scissor
snuffers. 1894, 4.5in (11.5cm)
long, H

Salvers

A pair of Irish William III sterling silver salvers, by Joseph Walker of Dublin. 1694, 10.5in (26.5cm) diam, E

1. Is it hallmarked in a line underneath the base?
2. Are the arms original?
3. Is the decoration chased (1740s) or engraved?
4. Is the border either moulded and applied, or cast?
5. Is the silver solid?
6. Has the border remained in good condition with no splitting?
7. Does it have three cast feet rather than one central one?

Salvers

The first commonly seen salvers date from the end of the 17thC and were used to present and serve food or drink. The earliest type had a central trumpet-shaped foot, resembling a *tazza*, but by the reign of George I (c1714) the central foot was replaced by three or more small feet. Most salvers are oval or circular. Unusual salver shapes, such as square and octofoil (a lobed variation of the octagonal form), are particularly sought after and valuable.

Trays or salvers

Nowadays, small salvers are occasionally described as waiters.

Decoration

Most salvers had a crest or coat of arms engraved in a decorative cartouche in the centre and were edged by a decorative border.

Beware

Many 18thC salvers were redecorated in the Victorian period. The chasing

An Irish salver, by Thomas Bolton of Dublin. 1728, 6.25in (16cm) wide, 8.5oz, D

is usually broader and the style of decoration in greater relief with more elaborate motifs than would be expected in the 18thC.

Regency salvers

Weight and quality are synonymous in Regency salvers; the most expensive are silver gilt. Chasing was extensive and many had large borders

An Irish George II salver, by 'CT' of Dublin. 1747, 7in (18cm) diam, 9oz, F

and paw feet. Other factors affecting the value of salvers are:
• Size – large salvers are rare and sought after.
• Sets – salvers were often made in pairs or larger numbers; a pair is worth more than twice a single, the premium increasing with age.

Removal of arms

Removed or re-engraved arms reduce value considerably.

Salvers

A salver, by William Peaston of London, with a shell and scroll rim, set on three scroll feet. 1755, 12.5in (32cm) diam, 32.5oz, G

A pair of George III salvers, by Parker & Wakelin of London, the edge with gadroon and Rococo shell and leaf scroll and with a Rococo engraved band with scenes in the Louis XV picturesque style representing the Four Elements. 1761, 13.75in (35cm) diam, 91.25oz, D

A George III salver, by Richard Williams of Dublin. It is not unusual to find Irish silver undated as 40 per cent of Irish silver has no date. The border of shells in this configuration is particular to Ireland. c1770, 14.5in (37cm) diam, D

A George III salver, by James Scott of Dublin, applied with a pierced die-stamped trailing vine border, the centre engraved with an armorial, on three satyr-mask feet. 1808, 11in (28cm) diam, 30oz, C

An American salver, by Lincoln & Reed of Boston, MA, on three scrolled feet, the rim cast with shells and 'C'-scrolls, the body etched with heraldic crest. c1840, 13.25in (33.5cm) diam, 32oz, F

A Victorian salver, by Samuel Smith of London, engraved with a crest and ribbon motto 'Jamais Arriere', with a flatchased surround of flowers and foliate scrolls. 1866, 10.5in (26.5cm) diam, 20.25oz, G

A late Victorian salver, by William Gibson & John Langman of London, with a Chippendale border, centrally engraved with the crest of Fane, on six cast scroll feet. 1897, 26in (66cm) diam, 202.25oz, D

An Arts and Crafts salver, by William George Connell of London, the rim embossed with flower heads and leaves on a matted ground. 1901, 12in (30.5cm) diam, 19oz, G

Trays

A royal presentation tray, to H. R. H. Ernest Augustus, Duke of Cumberland, by Digby Scott & Benjamin Smith of London. 1805, 29.5in (75cm) wide, 250oz, A+++

1. Is the tray marked in a line under the base with a large set of hallmarks?
2. Are the feet in proportion to the tray?
3. Is there a crest or coat of arms?
4. Does the border conform with the period of the tray?
5. If there is an engraved band, is this in keeping with the date of the tray?
6. Have the feet been pushed into the flat metal surface of the tray?

Trays

Trays usually have handles while salvers do not. Few trays were made before the 1780s and most early examples are oval in shape. Trays became more elaborate in the 19thC. Also like salvers, trays usually have feet. These need to be solid to bear the weight of the metal.

Armorials

Almost all trays are engraved with a coat of arms, crest or inscription. If a crest has been removed from the

A George III tray, by Thomas Hannam & John Crouch II of London. c1804, 25.5in (65cm) wide, 105oz, E

A George III tray, by William Bennett of London. 1802, 20in (51cm) wide, 56oz, F

centre of a tray there will be a dip in the metal and the value of the piece will be significantly reduced. Trays are usually thick enough for the indentation to be concealed by hammering it through to the back, leaving the surface flat. It is easier to

feel the dips with the fingertips.
• Very few trays are simply centred by a crest because arms and a cartouche fill the space far more satisfactorily.
• By the start of the 19thC taking tea and coffee with friends was a very popular pastime. This led to a need for larger trays to hold everything that was put on them. Square shapes, elaborate borders and chased decoration typify trays of the William IV period and presage later Victorian examples. Trays of this date are always relatively large and are highly sought-after by collectors.

Beware

Occasionally, meat dishes with handles that have been added will be sold as trays. These can usually be identified by their lack of feet and also by the fact that the handles are not integral to the body.

Trays

*A late 18thC Italian tray,
with gadrooned rim and
two handles, 'BC' of Venice
hallmark. 21in (53cm)
long, 49oz, E*

*An early 19thC footed tray, by Taylor &
Hinsdale of New York, NY, inscribed 'M.
Willett'. This tray was owned by Col. Willett.
He gained fame as a Sons of Liberty member
when he seized arms from the British as they
attempted to flee New York City. 20.25in
(51.5cm) diam, 85.5oz, D*

*A three-part plateau, by Robert Garrard of
London, with rounded end pieces flanking a
rectangular centre section, the end sections
with a single toupie foot, the centre section
with four further legs with patera bosses.
1871, 25.5in (65cm) wide, B*

*A Victorian presentation wine
tray, by Martin, Hall & Co.
of London, with a gadrooned
rim, on four nub feet, with
ebony handle-grips. 1881, 29in
(73.5cm) long, 159oz, F*

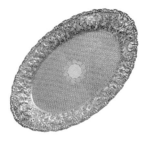

*A silver bread tray, by A. Jacobi & Co.,
retailed by James R. Armiger of Baltimore,
MD, with chased floral-decorated repoussé
sides inside a cast-applied scroll and shell
edge. 1893-5, 14in (35.5cm) wide, F*

*A drinks tray, by Thomas Bradbury &
Sons of Sheffield, cast and applied wavy
gadrooned rim with pierced and engraved
foliate gallery, raised on eight cast scroll
feet. 1895, 23in (58.5cm) wide, 109oz, F*

*A Gorham tray, of shaped oval
form with a reeded border,
monogrammed. 1917, 23in
(58.5cm) wide, F*

*A c1920s Georg
Jensen silver pin
tray. 10.25in (26cm)
long, E*

Cruet frames

A George III Warwick cruet, by Samuel Wood of London.
1754, 9in (23cm) high, 78.25oz, E

1. Is the frame marked underneath the base of the body?
2. Are the same marks visible on the bottles, caster and covers?
3. Is the handle marked with at least a lion passant and maker's mark?
4. If there is a crest, is it the same on both casters and frame?
5. Is there any damage to the piercing on the casters?
6. Are the bottles intact, and the same size?
7. Are the handles and feet in good condition?

Cruet frames

The earliest cruets were made in the 1720s. The Warwick frame opposite comprises a set of three casters – to hold salt, mustard and pepper – and two glass bottles for oil and vinegar. By the end of the 18thC the number of bottles and casters in a set had risen to eight or even ten in a frame to hold soy and other exotic sauces. Originally, rectangular or crescent-shaped sauce labels (small versions of wine labels) would have hung round the necks of the bottles. Shapes of bottles and casters vary according to the date they were made.

Marks

The body should have a full set of hallmarks; if the handle unscrews, it should be part-marked. Bottle mounts are often not marked before 1784, but should be marked thereafter. All the detachable pieces

A George III cruet frame, by William Abdy of London. 1780, 7in (18cm) wide, stand 12oz, E

– base, frame, tops and handle – should have matching marks. By the third quarter of the 18thC oil and vinegar bottles were made with decorative handles and hinged covers and casters had glass bodies.

Bottles

Bottles and their frames frequently become separated and are sold individually – make sure to check.

A late George II cruet frame, by Jabez Daniell & James Mince of London. 1759, 8.5in (21.5cm) high, F

Cruet frames

A George III six-bottle cruet frame, by Paul Storr of London, the stand raised on lily cast feet, the frame supported on paw-foot legs; each bottle with a sterling collar, two with sterling labels 'Harvey' and 'Soy'; three stoppers with silver-gilt condiment spoons. 1810, 11.75in (30cm) long, 29oz, E

A Regency cruet stand, by William Southey of London, with eight bottles, the stem with lion's head and leaf-cast loop handle, on paw feet. 1812, 14.5in (37cm) long, 52oz, D

A George IV egg cruet, by Benjamin Smith of London, the shaped gadroon-edge frame supporting eight egg cups below a cut glass bowl. 1827, 9in (23cm) high, F

A William IV egg cruet set, by the Barnards of London, acanthus-sheathed upswept stem to oval-ring handle, supporting six pedestal semi-ovoid egg cups. 1830, 9in (23cm) high, 37oz, F

A 'Warwick' cruet, by Edward I, Edward II,
James & William Barnard of London, the
frame of four eagle's masks, acanthus and
claw-and-ball feet, fitted with three lidded
casters, two silver-mounted cut-glass bottles.
1838-9, 15.25in (39cm) high, 110oz, B

A five-bottle condiment
cruet, by George Fox of
London, of cinque foil shape,
the centre stem with Rococo
scroll and shell lift. 1860, 8in
(20.5cm) high, 15.5oz, H

A late 19thC German silver and glass cruet
set, by C. Haub of Hanau, of two-bottle form
with all-over foliate decoration, the holder
stamped '935', the bottle mounts '950'.
10.5in (26.5cm) high, 15.75oz, H

A French Art Deco
cruet set, in silver
and crystal. c1930,
8in (20.5cm)
high, F

Salt cellars

A pair of George II salt cellars, by David & Robert Hennell of London. 1759, 3.5in (9cm) long, 8oz, H

1. Is the salt cellar marked in a group under the base?
2. Is the body free from any salt corrosion?
3. Are the feet not pushed into the body?
4. Do the feet sit squarely on the table? Is there any damage at the joints?
5. Does it have a well-fitting blue glass liner?
6. Is it one of a pair or a larger set? (Single ones are far less sought zafter.)
7. Is any chased decoration applied?

Salt cellars

Salt cellars were produced in large numbers from the 18thC onwards, in pairs or larger sets. Salts with pierced bodies raised on four feet were made in large numbers from the 1750s,

A pair of George III salt cellars, by WC, of London. 1770, 3.25in (8cm) long, 5.5oz, H

occasionally with matching mustard pots. They remain easily available and are relatively inexpensive, depending on quality. The pair opposite are of reasonable quality with an attractive wavy rim (mirrored by the liner) and good quality claw-and-ball feet.

• This type of salt cellar is prone to split rims, damaged piercing and cracked or broken feet, so always check carefully.

Desirable salt cellars from the 1790s will feature:

• attractive fluted body
• octagonal shape
• end grips
• gilded interior (can be used without a liner).

One drawback of this style is the potential weakness at the point where the foot joins the body and this should be checked for splits.

Marks

Trenchers are usually marked in a line under the bowls; marks may be badly worn. Marks on late 18thC salt cellars may be on each corner or in a line. These dishes are sometimes sold on their own as sweetmeat dishes. They are much more valuable if they retain the original glass liners. Salts of this type are usually of reasonable weight and can be attractive if sold with their glass holder as part of a set. Individually and without their liners they are less interesting.

A set of Irish salt cellars, by Michael Walsh of Dublin. c1780, 4in (10cm) long, 13oz, E

Salt cellars

A George III navette pedestal salt cellar, by William Plummer of London, with scroll handles, rope and twist rim, engraved with a crest and 'WL'. c1782, 12.5cm (5in) long, 3.25oz, J

A George III salt cellar, by William Sumner of London, with reeded loop handles and borders, engraved with a monogram. 1792, 6in (15.5cm) long, 3oz, J

A set of George III salt cellars, by Paul Storr of London, applied with oak leaves and acorns, the handles as branches, on acanthus leaf and shell scroll bracket feet. 1816, 5.5in (14cm) wide, 44oz, A

A pair of salt cellars, by Charters, Cann & Dunn and retailed by John & James Cox, both of New York, the trefoil bowl on three cast and chased mask-headed scroll feet. c1848–53, 3in (7.5cm) wide, G

A salt cellar, by E. & J. Barnard of London, in the form of a duck, with a silver-gilt interior, marked beneath 'Thomas's, Bond St, London'. 1862, 4.75in (12cm) long, 10oz, G

A late Victorian pedestal salt cellar, of Monteith form, with original spoon, London. 1887, 3in (7.5cm) wide, 3oz, J

A Russian salt cellar, by Ovchinnikov of Moscow, assay master Viktor Savinkov, designed as a woven sack, signed in Cyrillic beneath an Imperial eagle warrant, 84 zolotnik mark. 1873, 4in (10cm) long, G

A pair of late 19thC Indian colonial silver-mounted salt cellars, the foliate-carved coconut shell bodies raised on three ball feet. 3.5in (9cm) long, J

75

Pepper casters

A George III pepper pot, maker's mark unidentified,
London. 1761, 5in (12.5cm) high, 4oz, J

1. Is the caster marked in a group under the base?
2. Are there also marks on the cover?
3. Has the piercing remained intact?
4. Is the finial in good, unrestored condition?
5. If there is a coat of arms, is it contemporary with the date of the caster?
6. Does the join between foot and body seem secure?
7. Is the caster a tall bulbous shape?

Pepper casters

Casters were made from the late 17thC, frequently in sets of three, with one large and two smaller casters. The larger caster was used for sugar; smaller ones were for pepper. Casters diminished in popularity towards the end of the 18thC, when they were replaced by cruets.

Marks

Marks should be found on both the body and the cover. The body tends to be marked in a group under the base, although early ones and those from the late 18thC are sometimes marked in a straight line on the body. The cover is usually marked with a lion passant and possibly a maker's mark. Casters like the one below are termed kitchen peppers because they have a handle to enable the cook to season the food more easily. Peppers of this distinctive shape date from before c1730 and are relatively scarce. Bun peppers, so-called because of the shape of the cover, were produced throughout the 18thC; the one below was made in 1742 by William Garrard, a prolific maker. Bun peppers are smaller than most others, measuring about 3in (7.5cm), and are among the least expensive casters. Bun peppers are usually marked in the piercing. As there is no bezel on

A George II bun pepper pot, by William Garrard of London. 1742, 2.5in (6.5cm) high, 3oz, J

the cover, the tops fall off easily, and many were lost and replaced. If the cover is not contemporary with the base the pepper is best avoided.

Spoons

Mustard spoons were made by spoonmakers, a specific trade distinct from makers of mustard pots. Spoons were usually bought separately, but they were sometimes engraved to match the pot.

A George I kitchen pepper, by James Godwin of London. 1719, 3in (7.5cm) high, G

Pepper casters

A George II provincial pepperette, of baluster form, by Isaac Cookson of Newcastle. c1750, 3.5in (9cm) high, J

A George III bun pepper, London mark, with a stepped and reeded body, monogrammed. 1780, 2.75in (7cm) high, 1oz, J

A George III kitchen pepper pot, by John Emes of London, of plain cylindrical form, with domed pull-off cover and scroll handle. 1804, 2.5in (6.5cm) high, 2oz, J

A pair of George III pepper pots, by John Shaw of Birmingham, the pull-off pierced covers with Gothic influence. 1806, 5in (12.5cm) high, 4oz, J

A pepper mill, by Sampson Mordan of London, modelled as an 18thC caster, of octagonal baluster form. 1880, 5in (12.5cm) high, H

A novelty pepperette, by C. Saunders & F. Shepherd of Chester, in the form of a miniature side-handle coffee pot. 1896, 1.75in (4.5cm) high, J

An Edwardian novelty pepper pot, by William Hornby of London, modelled as a wren, with pull-off cover. 1906, 1.5in (4cm) high, J

A novelty pepper pot, by Sebastian Garrard of London, modelled as a seated mastiff, with pull-off pierced cover. 1922, 2.5in (6.5cm) high, 3.5oz, F

Mustard pots

A George III mustard pot, by Peter & Ann Bateman of London,
with a blue glass liner. 1799, 3.5in (8.5cm) high, 2oz, G

1. Does the piece bear a full set of hallmarks in a line on the body?
2. Is there a maker's mark and lion passant on the cover?
3. If the pot was made after 1784, is there also a sovereign's head mark?
4. Does the liner fit well?
5. Has the finial remained intact? (If it has been torn off the value is reduced.)
6. Is the hinge in a good state of repair?
7. Does the silver on the side or cover seem thinner than the rest of the body? (This could indicate an erased crest and reduces value.)

Mustard Pots

Mustard pots became popular from c1765–70. Early pots were usually fitted with blue glass liners, which were easier to wash than silver. Condiment sets with matching mustard, salt and pepper were not made until the late Victorian period. Octagonal pots command a premium. Bright-cut engraved decoration of this type also boosts the value. Also popular with today's collectors are figural and novelty pots.

Marks

The body should have a full set of hallmarks, either in a group on the base, in a line on the body or in a curve round the base. The lids should be separately marked with maker's mark and lion passant and pieces that were made after 1784 should also have the sovereign's head.

Liners

Original liners have

A George III drum mustard pot, maker's mark 'M', London, gilt interior and blue glass liner. 1812, 2.75in (7cm) high, 6oz, G

An early 19thC German pierced mustard pot, by 'I.G.S', of Augsburg. c1800, 5in (12.5cm) high, 5oz, H

a large star cut in the base. Damage piercing and open work should always be checked carefully for damage. Other areas of potential weakness are:

• The hinge – it may have been weakened.

• The handle – it can pull away from body.

• The body – may be fragile because areas have been cut away and therefore is vulnerable to damage.

Beware

Some mustard pots have been converted from egg cups or salt cellars and these are far less desirable. Ovoid pots, or those on three feet, and any pot that does not have cover marks should be avoided.

Mustard pots

A Scottish provincial mustard pot, by
A. McLeod of Inverness, the reticulated
sides with arched design with engraved
detail. c1830, 3in (7.5cm) high, 3.5oz, E

A mustard pot, by James Dixon & Sons
of Sheffield, with embossed foliate scroll
decoration, and engraved with a crest. 1839,
5in (12.5cm) high, 8oz, G

A rare novelty mustard pot, by James
Barclay Hennell of London, in the form of
a boar, with original spoon, the terminal
forming his tail. 1880, 4in (10cm) long,
3.5oz, D

A pair of American novelty mustard
pots, by R. Blackington & Co., North
Attleboro, MA, modelled as military
side drums. c1900, 3.5in (9cm) high,
8.25oz, J

An Arts and Crafts mustard pot by The Guild of Handicraft Ltd of London, the domed hinged lid with a flower-head finial, mounted with a cornelian. 1902, 2.75in (7cm) high, J

A Liberty & Co. three-piece cruet set, each set with turquoise cabochons, marks for Birmingham. c1917, 2in (5cm) high, H

A George V novelty mustard pot, by C. Saunders & F. Shepherd of London, in the form of 'Humpty Dumpty', with blue glass liner and spoon. 1924–5, 1.75in (4.5cm) high, 0.5oz, H

A tankard-shaped mustard pot, for Reid & Son Ltd of Newcastle upon Tyne, hallmark for Sheffield. 1936, 2.5in (6.5cm) high, H

Decorative tableware

Among some of the more expensive items of silver available to the collector are the large decorative items that were bought by the rich largely as an external show of wealth. These are all very popular today because they can be used as attractive objects to display on a large table. Objects range from exuberant epergnes and centrepieces to large baskets, punch bowls and monteiths. Because these were mainly large and expensive items even when made, many were produced as presentation pieces and bear an inscription to this effect. Unfortunately, unless the inscription is particularly interesting, the value of the piece will be significantly lower.

Epergnes generally have a central basket and several smaller bowls. Early examples have candle sockets that are interchangeable with the smaller baskets. The first epergnes were made in the second quarter of the 18thC and their production coincided with the rise in popularity of the Rococo-style and the return to fashion of Chinese motifs first used in the 1680s. Epergnes were always highly decorative, and swirling naturalistic motifs and Chinese masks were applied with enthusiasm – there are even examples with pagoda roofs hung with bells. Most of them were originally supplied with wooden boxes to protect them when not in use.

Epergnes were replaced later in the 18thC with the centrepiece, which at first was made to stand on its own in the centre of the table, but which later became the focal point of an entire decorative scheme of smaller pieces placed at intervals down the table. By the end of the century many centrepieces were made in Sheffield plate, which made them more affordable. Their liners are often missing, and because they were usually frosted and engraved, they are hard to copy today. They can add considerably to the decorative effect of a centrepiece and an obvious replacement will lower the value.

Mirror plateaus – glass trays used to mirror the light – were seldom made at exactly the same time as the centrepiece, but they add greatly to the decorative effect and are an attractive addition. They are also sought after on their own,

particularly for displaying celebration cakes. Silver baskets were first produced in the 1730s, and although early ones are rare, available in large numbers are those dating from the mid-18thC onwards. Curiously, they seem to be almost exclusively a British idea, although some were produced in the United States. Most are pierced, and as they were in daily use for a long time it is important to check for damage.

Irish silver is always popular, as evidenced by the basket by William Nowlan of Dublin (above) who worked on Whitefriar Street and was active from 1811 to 1835. With the embossed foliate scroll and bird decoration on the matted ground and the handle with caryatid supports, it is typical of the decorative baskets produced at this period. Particularly from the end of the 18thC, baskets were made with simple wirework sides, or (on those in the more usual oval shape) wirework sides overlaid with sheafs of corn – both types are believed to have been for bread rather than fruit or cakes. Baskets tended to get lighter over a period of time.

This is probably due to an increase in demand from the less wealthy section of the market. They also became more shallow. Any baskets without handles should be checked carefully to make sure a handle has not been removed.

A number of grand silver-gilt examples were produced in the Regency period, which are very expensive today. Baskets are popular as they can display fruit attractively in the centre of a large table.

Punch bowls and monteiths both originated in the 1680s. Monteiths were used for serving iced drinks and were fashionable for about 50 years until they had a revival in the late 19thC. Like some punch bowls they have handles, probably made necessary for carrying the bowls due to the condensation that formed on the outside. Occasionally, monteiths without their rims are sold as punch bowls but this is usually apparent because a monteith has a plain wire

A late Victorian punch bowl, by Walker & Hall of Sheffield. 1898, 10in (25.5cm) diam, 41oz, F

rim on which the collar sits and a punch bowl does not. Punch bowls also tend to be deeper.

From the middle of the 17thC until the end of the 19thC, the shared bowl of punch was the undisputed king of mixed drinks.

In the beginning, punch was a simple mixture of five ingredients: citrus juice, sugar, water, spice – often nutmeg or ambergris – and, of course, alcohol. Batavia arrack, from the Dutch East Indies, was the preferred spirit, but Caribbean rum and French brandy were also in demand.

Punch seems to have been mixed in the dining room and the bowl required a number of accessories. Most obvious is the ladle. This initially had a silver handle, but later it was wood, and then whale bone, when it also became much smaller. Other accessories included orange strainers, which had wide handles to go over the bowl, but few of these have survived. Sugar was also a necessity in the process and the early sugar bowls without lids were developed at this time.

Differences between porringers and caudle cups seem to be blurred, and both were designed to hold warm liquid. If caudle cups are defined as having baluster bodies their production was confined to the late 17thC. The porringer has a far longer lifespan and many of those seen today date from the 18thC. The American porringer is quite a different vessel to the British one, and in Britain is rather improbably called a 'bleeding bowl'.

A number of spout cups were produced as an alternative to the caudle cup. These are now very rare and seem to have been used for feeding the elderly and infirm.

Centrepieces are as variable as the styles of the period in which they were made, from early examples that involved candelabrum to later examples with leaf-cast scrolled branches supporting bowls and the Art Nouveau piece below with nymphs and berried foliage.

A William Hutton & Sons Ltd silver centrepiece, by Kate Harris, London. 1899, 19.5in (50cm) high, D

Epergnes

A George III epergne, by Thomas Pitts of London, with central William IV additions by Joseph Craddock of London. 1761 and 1830, 18.5in (47cm) high, 193.75oz, C

1. Are the body and central basket fully marked with the same set of marks?
2. Do all the other component parts (such as branches, baskets and swing handles) have some marks?
3. Is the piercing in good condition?
4. Are the swags or branches free from repairs? (If they have been snapped and soldered the piece is devalued.)
5. Are the feet undamaged?
6. Do any crests or coats of arms match on all the dishes? (Those with different crests are very suspect.)

Epergnes

Epergnes first appeared towards the middle of the 18thC. They were placed in the centre of grand dinner tables to hold fruit and sweetmeats. Rare and expensive epergnes tend to get larger and wider as the century progresses; the early pieces from c1730 are relatively compact. Mid-18thC versions tend to have four side baskets along with a larger central one.

Decoration

The styles and decoration of epergnes reflects contemporary styles and fashions in other types of silver and applied arts of the period.

Glass liners

Glass liners – as seen on the epergne made by Thomas Pitts in 1768 (right) – were a necessary addition

to epergnes from the third quarter of the 18thC.

Regency epergnes

Heavy florid shapes, with large low feet became fashionable in the early

A George III epergne, by Thomas Pitts of London. 1768, 38in (15in) high, B

19thC. Damage to the glass bowls, or the replacement of bowls on Regency epergnes will reduce the value dramatically. But Regency glass is often easier to replace than Victorian glass, which is frequently frosted and engraved. This is virtually impossible to match with existing glass today – copying a cut-glass bowl is far easier.

Marks

The body and central basket should have a full set of hallmarks. All the other parts should be part-marked, with the lion passant, maker's mark and, from 1784, the sovereign mark.

A Georgian epergne, by Butty & Dumée of London. 1767, 13in (33cm) high, 74.5oz, C

Epergnes

A George III epergne, by William Pitts of London, the central pierced boat-shaped basket centred by a cartouche engraved with an heraldic shield, raised on four reeded legs ending on paw feet. 1800, 25.5in (65cm) wide, 92oz, B

A George III epergne, by John Plimmer of London, the openwork frame centred by a pierced boat-shaped semi-lobed basket, surrounded by eight acanthus-decorated scroll branches. c1804, 13.25in (33.5cm) high, 114oz, B

A George III epergne, by Thomas Holland of London, the cut-glass bowl with a barbed rim supported by a frame cast with female terms and plumes. 1804, 11.75in (30cm) high, 55oz, C

A George III-style epergne, by Joshua Vander of London, after a design by Thomas Pitts, the foliate-chased swag aprons surmounted by a basket, with four supporting pierced baskets, and four hanging. 1890, 26in (66cm) high, B

*An Indian colonial epergne,
marked 'T.90', foliate chased
throughout and inscribed within
a shield cartouche 'From Vakil
Brothers'. c1890, 13in (33cm)
high, 26oz, H*

*An epergne, by Walker &
Hall of Sheffield, the central
trumpet-shaped vase flanked
by three small vases and
three baskets. 1903, 16in
(40.5cm) high, E*

*A George V epergne, by James Deakin &
Sons of Sheffield, with four detachable,
tapered, square-shaped vases. 1914, 14in
(35.5cm) high, 9oz, H*

*A George V epergne, maker's/retailer's mark
D & B of Birmingham, the central trumpet vase
issuing two scroll arms, each with a hanging
basket. 1925, 10.25in (26cm) high, 22oz, H*

Centrepieces

*A Regency ten-light
'Huntly Testimonial'
candelabrum centrepiece,
by Paul Storr for Rundell,
Bridge & Rundell of
London. 1814, 39.75in
(101cm) high, 847oz, A++*

1. Is it marked on every detachable part (body, figures, sconces, branches, base etc.)?
2. Is each individual branch numbered or marked with identical dots?
3. Are all parts of the decoration intact?
4. If there is a mirror plateau, is it silver? (It could be electroplate.)
5. If the mirror plateau is not silver, does it match the centrepiece?

Centrepieces

The epergne was replaced by the centrepiece in the late 18thC. They tend to have fewer side bowls than epergnes. The bowl was either solid silver or pierced, in which case it had a glass liner. They were made both with and without candlesticks and had a central bowl for holding fruit. Centrepieces came in fitted wooden boxes with baize-lined compartments for the arms but, often

A German centrepiece on stand, by G. Hossauer of Berlin. c1853, 18.5in (47cm) high, 145.5oz, D

relatively simple in design. By the second half of the 19thC centrepieces were often reduced to one central basket on a stand without any fitments for candles. Centrepieces became increasingly shorter and soon developed into dessert stands, which replaced centrepieces at the end of the century.

Care

Centrepieces are virtually impossible to clean properly on a regular basis. It would be advisable to have them professionally cleaned and then covered with a protecting surface, which will prevent them from tarnishing. It is best, therefore, to then handle them only with protective gloves.

A centrepiece, by Matthew Boulton of Birmingham. 1839, 21.75in (55cm) high, 152oz, D

kept in dark and damp cellars, very few have survived the passage of time. Centrepieces from the 1820s were

Centrepieces

A centrepiece, by Thomas Bradbury & Sons, London, the stem in the form of a grape vine. c1869, 12in (30.5cm) high, 26.5oz, F

A pair of Art Nouveau centrepieces, marked 'Lazarus Posen Veuve', with German government mark, with male and female figures supporting the shellwork bowl. 1888, 14in (35.5cm) high, 157oz, B

A late 19thC Austrian rock-crystal and silver-gilt centrepiece, with Vienna greyhound hallmark. 1872–1922, 4.75in (12cm) high, 6.25oz, D

An Austrian centrepiece, by Franz Rumwolf, with Vienna Diana hallmark. 1872–1922, 9in (23cm) high, 36oz, E

A Chinese centrepiece, a punch mark for Yi Chang, formed as four palm trees issuing from a vase. c1900, 16.75in (42.5cm) high, D

An Austrian Rococo Revival centrepiece, by J. C. Klinkosch, with Vienna Diana hallmark. 1872–1922, 18in (46cm) high, 117oz, C

A German silver and glass centrepiece, with German stamp. c1900, 8.75in (22cm) high, F

A pair of early 20thC silver-gilt, bronze and faux hardstone centrepieces, of North American interest. 32in (81cm) high, B

Baskets

A George II silver basket, by Paul de Lamerie of London.
1739, 14in (35.5cm) wide, A+++

1. Is the basket marked on the top in the piercing or in a straight line underneath?
2. Is the handle part-marked to match?
3. If there is still a coat of arms present in the base of the basket does it conform in style to the date of the basket?
4. Is any bright-cut or pierced decoration in good condition?
5. Has the handle remained intact?

Baskets

Baskets became fashionable from c1730 onwards and were placed in the centre of a table to hold fruit, bread, cakes or sweetmeats. Though relatively expensive items they were produced in large numbers. Styles and shapes vary, but up until the end of the 18thC most had some form of pierced decoration, which can be

A George III pierced basket, by William Plummer of London. 1760, 14.5in (37cm) wide, E

vulnerable to damage and should be carefully examined. Baskets often stand on a rimmed foot; others have separate bases and these should be fully marked, with part marks on the body and handle.

Chinoiserie decoration is particularly sought after. It is not very common on baskets and adds about 50 per cent to their value.

The most commonly seen baskets are those dating from the late 18thC, of oval shape with swing handle and pierced decoration.

Marks

18thC baskets may be marked in a line on one of the straight lines of the piercing. Basket handles should also be marked to correspond with those on the body.

Condition

Any basket that stands on four feet should be checked, as the feet are easily pushed up through the body and prone to cracking. Later, baskets with a pierced apron support became popular. These pieces will also be vulnerable to damage.

A George III bread basket, by Kerr & Dempster of Edinburgh. 1768–69, 13in (33cm) wide, 35oz, E

Baskets

*A Dutch sweetmeat basket, by Johannes
Schiotling of Amsterdam, the body pierced
and engraved with geometrical patterns,
and applied with garlands and ribbon-tied
medallions with double portraits. 1777, 7in
(18cm) wide, 11oz, C*

*A Regency basket, by
William Bateman of
London, the sides with
foliate embossed and
chased decoration. 1815,
13in (33cm) wide, F*

*A cake basket, by Harvey Lewis of
Philadelphia, PA, heavily chased with
rosettes, shells and leaves and a narrow
'thread and shell' inner edge. c1815, 10.25in
(26cm) diam, 33oz, A*

*A pair of bread baskets, by Howard & Co.
of New York, pierced overall with scrolls
and cartouche-form pierced handles, on
four scroll feet. c1900, 11.5in (29cm) wide,
39oz, G*

A basket, by William Hutton
& Sons of Sheffield, with a
reticulated rim and pierced sides
centred by a shield, raised on a
pierced oval foot. 1901, 14.5in
(37cm) long, 26oz, G

A basket, by Charles Stuart
Harris of London, with pierced
decoration and embossed with
rosettes and swags, on four shell
feet. 1902, 14in (35.5cm) long,
50oz, E

An American Art Nouveau footed
centre bowl, by Gorham Mfg Co.,
Providence, RI, the rim decorated
with floral baskets. c1905, 10.5in
(26.5cm) wide G

A basket, by Josef Hoffmann for
Wiener Werkstätte, with ivory handle,
with Vienna Diana hallmark. Only
seven of these were made. c1905,
10.25in (26cm) wide, A+

Punch bowls

A Queen Anne punch bowl, by Samuel Wastell of London.
1703, 9.5in (24cm) diam, 25oz, E

1. Is the bowl marked in a group underneath?
2. Is there a large contemporary coat of arms? (A plain surface, or anything small, such as a crest, would be suspect.)
3. Does the bowl have an elaborate cartouche? Are the arms contemporary with the cartouche?
4. Has it been left relatively unpolished so that the attractive patina has not been removed?
5. Is there any evidence of any engraving having been removed?
6. Is there an absence of splits round the rim?

Punch bowls

The earliest punch bowls date from the last quarter of the 17thC when punch, a drink made from claret, brandy and spices, was introduced to

A punch bowl, by Peter, Ann & William Bateman of London. c1804, 14.5in (37cm) diam, D

Britain from India. After c1730, glass replaced silver, and any silver punch bowls after this date tend to have been made as prizes.

Collecting

Early punch bowls are very expensive, and today are bought primarily for decorative purposes, as a centrepiece, rather than for use. Appearances at auction are infrequent as they were not made in large quantities because of their size. Many punch bowls were made without handles, which must have made them very awkward to move when full. Perhaps this confirms that punch was made and distributed in one place: the dining room.

Bowls became gradually broader and shallower with a taller rim. They became progressively larger over the years and were made in even smaller quantities than previously.

Marks

Early bowls are usually marked in a straight line along the side. Most 18thC examples are marked underneath in the points of a compass. Later bowls are marked on the side again. Marks underneath should be safe, but marks on the side of a large plain surface may be rubbed away by over-zealous cleaning. If marked underneath, make sure the marks have not been let in.

A 19thC repoussé punch bowl, by The Loring Andrews Co., Cincinnati, OH. 11.75in (30cm) wide, E

Punch bowls

A punch bowl, by
Charles Stuart
Harris of London.
1893, 15in (38cm)
diam, E

A pedestal punch bowl, by Charles Stuart
Harris of London, the half spiralling
lobed body alternating with embossed
foliate swags. c1897, 15.75in (40cm)
diam, 86.7oz, E

An American punch bowl, by
Dominick & Haff, retailed by
Frank Herschede, with a foliate
and scroll cast rim. c1900, 11.5in
(29cm) diam, 52oz, F

A punch bowl, the sides chased
with rocaille scrolls and
flowers, London hallmarks,
maker's mark worn. c1901, 14in
(35.5cm) high, F

A punch bowl, cover and ladle, by Goldsmiths & Silversmiths Company of London, the bowl with planished finish and three open curved supports, with urn finial. 1904, 8.75in (22cm) diam, 77.5oz, E

A Russian Imperial presentation punch set, to Rear Admiral Charles Henry Davis, U.S.N., Mikhail Grachev, the punch bowl modelled as a stylized Viking longship. 1905, bowl 21in (53cm) wide, 232oz, A+

A montieth bowl, by Edward Barnard & Sons of London, the rim with 'C'-scroll notches centred by putti masks, the sides with lion-headed armorial cartouches. 1906, 13.5in (34cm) diam, 108oz, D

An Old Newbury Crafters punch bowl and tray, retailed by Shreve, Crump & Low, Boston, MA, bowl raised on silver-framed blue enamel bars. c1970, tray 18.75in (47.5cm) diam 228oz, D

Bowls

*A Britannia silver bleeding bowl, by Charles Overing of
London. 1699, 5in (12.5cm) long, 4oz, E*

1. Is the bowl marked in a group underneath or round the rim?
2. Is there a contemporary coat of arms?
3. Is there any evidence of any engraving having been removed?
4. Has the bowl been left relatively unpolished so that it displays a
   good original patina?
5. If the bowl is a bleeding bowl, is the handle pierced?

Bowls

What the British call 'bleeding bowls' are called 'porringers' in the United States. They were made in the 17thC. Despite their medical name, it is most likely that they were used for food. Handles are always pierced, so check carefully for any splits.

The bowls should be marked on the outside of the rim or on the base. Any bowls that have a mark on the handle as well will command a premium.

A George I slop bowl, by James Kerr of Edinburgh. 1726, 5.5in (14cm) diam, 11.5oz, D

A Russian 'charka', by Semen Bogdanovich Nesterow. c1650, 6.25in (16cm) long, 5.25oz, A

Because they were not made in vast quantities they can be expensive – price depends upon the size and weight and the clarity of the marks. A crest on the handle will add value.

The Russian 'charka' on the left is a very rare early example in excellent condition. The rim has an engraving in Cyrillic. The fact that the bowl has parcel gilt decoration as well adds to its desirability. High-quality Russian silver and enamel is currently in great demand.

The slop bowl above by James Kerr is currently the earliest recorded Scottish three-footed slop/sugar bowl. Bowls with lion-headed paw feet were common in Ireland from c1735; this pre-dates that by a decade. Other makers who employed lion-headed paw feet include Paul de Lamerie. The large size of this bowl suggests it may have been used for slops, rather than sugar. Other sugar bowls of the period are smaller, partly due to the high cost of sugar.

Bowls

A Belgian silver bowl, maker's mark 'IDP' possibly for Jean-François Dupont, Liège. 1740, 6.75in (17cm) diam, D

An 18thC Channel Islands christening bowl, maker's mark 'GS' of Jersey, with handles engraved 'A*D*S*C'. c1730–79, 5in (12.5cm) wide, 2.5oz, E

A Liberty & Co. Aesthetic Movement bowl, with London marks and simulated Japanese mark. 1895, 4in (10cm) diam, H

A Chinese export bowl, by Wang Hing of Hong Kong, engraved with prunus blossom, bamboo and birds. c1896, 4.5in (11.5cm) diam, 5.5oz, F

An Arts and Crafts bowl, by Ramsden & Carr of London, having three wirework handles each punctuated with a red enamelled heart-shaped plaque. 1902, 4.75in (12cm) high, E

A bowl, by Tiffany & Co., New York, with an all-over floral arabesque pattern. 1906, 9in (23cm) diam, 32oz, F

A Georg Jensen, Copenhagen, silver bowl, with a typical stylized foliate base. 1933–44, 7.75in (19.5cm) diam, 22oz, E

An Arts and Crafts bowl, by Omar Ramsden of London, with spot-hammered decoration and pierced foliate border. c1935, 4.5in (11.5cm) wide, 6.75oz, F

Porringers

An early Charles II porringer, maker's mark 'IC' or 'IG'.
3.75in (9.5cm) diam, 4.5oz, E

1. Is there a band of lobing round the base?
2. Is there a corded girdle?
3. Are the handles flat strap if later, or cast if early?
4. Does it have a late 17thC-style cartouche?
5. Is the body gently flared?
6. Is it marked in a group underneath or on the side?
7. Is the decoration embossed? (Usually with acanthus or palm leaves.)

Porringers

A British porringer is a two-handled cylindrical cup, originally for porridge or gruel. They were made in large numbers from the mid-17thC to the middle of the 18thC. (For American poringers see p105.)

A 17thC American porringer, by John Hull of Boston, MA. 1624–83, 7.25in (18.5cm) wide, C

Caudle cups

Caudle cups, although similar to porringers, tend to have a baluster body, and were made for about 50 years in the second half of the 17thC. Caudle was a sweet mixture of wine and milk that was given to invalids and women in childbirth. The earliest porringers and caudle cups tend to have lids, later ones do not.

Condition

Check for holes in the chasing and any solder repairs in the decoration.

Look carefully at the handles for breaks. Because the handles are susceptible to straining they may have been pulled away from the body. In addition, porringers that sit directly on their bases are prone to damage as the metal underneath is sometimes thin. This type of damage has usually been repaired in the past with soft solder.

Marks

Caudle cups and porringers are marked in a group on the base, or in a straight line on the body near the lip by the handle. Some porringers and caudle cups were made with covers (including the piece illustrated below) and these should also be marked with a full set of hallmarks.

A porringer and cover, maker's mark 'WW' of London, embossed with lions and gazelles. 1668, 5.5in (14cm) high, 17.25oz, E

Porringers

A porringer, maker's mark 'IC' of London, the lower body chased with a frieze of stylized leaves below the pricked initials 'W.P'. 1675, 2.75in (7cm) high, 3.5oz, E

A pair of porringers, by John Ruslen of London, with foliate band above bands of palms and acanthus. 1691, 3.75in (9.5cm) high, 21oz, D

A porringer, by John Coney of Boston, MA. c1700, 8in (20.5cm) long, 7.5oz, D

A caudle cup, by William Twell of London. c1711, 3in (7.5cm) high, 5oz, F

A George I porringer, by William Darker of London, with a campana-shaped body. 1719, 5in (12.5cm) high, F

A colonial keyhole porringer, by Samuel Casey of Rhode Island, the handle engraved with block letters 'L*I*M'. 1723–73, 7.5in (19cm) long, E

A Tiffany & Co., New York, porringer, decorated with repoussé flora and fauna. c1880, 9in (23cm) wide, G

A Guild of Handicraft porringer and spoon, by Charles Robert Ashbee of London, set with green chrysoprase stones. 1902, 10.75in (27.5cm) wide, D

Drinking vessels

A huge number of drinking vessels – cups, tankards, goblets and jugs – have been made over the centuries; and they are very popular with collectors today. Most of those that have survived date from the 18thC onwards. Because they were generally very well used, condition is an important consideration – in particular, check any handles for straining, and the rims for splits. The earliest beakers date from before English silver was hallmarked and are fairly common both in Britain and on the Continent, although rare in the United States.

In Britain, beakers were produced on a large scale for domestic use. Most are very simple in design as befits such a utilitarian object. The exceptions are those beakers made for travelling grandees, produced predominantly on the Continent, which came in sets together with a knife, fork, spoon and spice box, assembled in a small silver case. These are always of very high quality with intricate engraving, and are highly sought after. In the United States, beakers with a pronounced Dutch influence in height and decoration were made in New York in the late 17thC. However, any later examples seem to have primarily been destined for church, rather than domestic use.

Tumbler cups, mostly broad and shallow, have always been popular with collectors because they are small, attractive and very tactile. The first ones were made in the 17thC and continued to be produced throughout the 18thC. However, they are rare and always command high prices. Many later tumbler cups were engraved and presented as race prizes.

Tankards were made in huge numbers both in England and the United States, although less were produced in Scotland and Ireland. Ones made from silver provided a popular and more robust alternative to drinking vessels made from stoneware. They seem to have been immune to changes in fashion and nearly all have a plain body with the simple addition of either a band of chased acanthus leaves or chinoiserie flat chasing at the base in the reign of Charles II, or a band of gadrooning at the end of the 17thC.

Wooden (or treen) peg tankards were

always popular in Scandinavia, as were the silver equivalents like the example below. It is a fairly typical example from the early 18thC, with its plain cylindrical body, engraved foliate border, pomegranate thumbpiece and feet, and scrolled handle with a classical mask and beading. Silver tankards from this period were status symbols and as such often had crests, coats of arms and inscriptions. This example is inscribed on the hinged lid 'Even Hansen/Anne Abraham/Daatter/1739'.

It was not until the Regency period that tankards became ornate, and then massive examples were produced in silver gilt to be given as presentation pieces. The Victorians, who disliked any plain surfaces, often added elaborate chasing in the form of animals, leaves and scrolls to earlier vessels. These tankards used to be virtually impossible to sell, but there is now a modest market for them if they are suitably attractive.

Tankards were frequently converted into more useful jugs during the 19thC but these tend to be less elegant than the original. To be legal the conversion must have later marks on any additions such as the spout.

A Norwegian peg tankard, maker's mark 'HNN'. c1735, 6.75in (17cm) high, 24oz, D

An interesting variation to the standard tankard is a design produced on the east coast of Britain, in York and to a lesser extent Newcastle. These show a Baltic influence.

They have pegs down the inside of the body to ensure fair shares for all at drinking parties. Tankards were important and expensive purchases and were recognized as being a tangible symbol of their owner's wealth; not surprisingly, most were therefore marked with their owner's arms or initials.

If the coat of arms on the side of a tankard is contemporary with the piece it will add significant value and interest to the tankard. If the arms have been erased the value will be reduced by at least a third.

The mug may seem a fairly obvious derivation of the tankard, but it did not appear in Britain until the late 17thC, and American examples were later still. Irish mugs are very rare. Like tankards, mugs were primarily plain until the end of the 18thC. In Victorian times small mugs were popular as gifts, especially at christenings, made in a huge variety of styles with profuse decoration. Very many early plain mugs have

114

A Charles II beaker, maker's mark of a goose in a dotted circle, London. c1679, 4in (10cm) high, 4.5oz, D

been later decorated; others have been converted into small cream jugs by the addition of a lip. As with most alterations these are likely to be illegal unless the additional parts have been hallmarked.

As with most silver, any deviation from the original object will subsequently cause a significant fall in the value.

Silver beakers can be found from the 16thC but they are rare before 1650. In the 1500s the beaker has been identified as the commonest form of drinking vessel in use. The term 'beaker' may be derived from the Greek *bikos* (earthenware jug), German *beker* or Old Norse *bikarr*. Beaker is the word traditionally used for a flat-based vessel without handles or a lid, from which liquid may be drunk or poured.

Examples of silver beakers from this period have a decorated, tapering cylindrical form such as the example opposite. It is embossed with various flowers and foliate decoration. It is not uncommon on silver that is of this period to be unable to identify the maker.

Some of the most decorative drinking vessels are 18thC goblets. Bright-cut examples made in the 1790s, in particular, can command substantial prices if they were still in pristine condition. Unlike mugs, it would be difficult to decorate a goblet at a later date as most already have some form of engraving.

Those produced throughout the Victorian era were particularly fancy, when they are sometimes made with matching jugs.

A later alternative to the tankard was the beer jug, produced in the 18thC. Beer jugs were expensive when new, despite the fact that most of them were plain. More elaborate exceptions are early jugs with cut-card decoration round the spout and base, and some very elegant and restrained Neo-classical jugs from the 1780s by such makers as Boulton and Fothergill. Victorian jugs had finer decoration on the body and were made for wine rather than beer.

A. J. C. Klinkosch goblet, Vienna, model no 11427, marked 'JCK' and '800'. c1922, 10in (25.5cm) high, 12oz, E

115

Beakers

*A Charles II beaker, maker's mark of a goose in a dotted
circle, London, embossed with flowers, prick dot initialled
'EAT 1680'. c1679, 4in (10cm) high, 4.5oz, D*

1. Is it marked in a group underneath the base?
2. Does it have a separate reeded foot?
3. Is the cylindrical body slightly flared at the lip?
4. Is there a leafy band of chased or engraved decoration round the
    top of the beaker?
5. Is the rim free from splits?
6. Does it have an original crest or coat of arms?

Beakers

Early beakers often had lids. After the Reformation beakers were occasionally used as communion cups and many true communion cups from the period will have a beaker-shaped bowl.

Form changes very little, although 16thC and early 17thC examples tend to be taller with a slightly broader base than later ones.

Decoration

Beakers are usually quite plain apart from a crest or coat of arms, although those dating from the reign of Charles II often have chased decoration of leaves and flowers, as in the main image shown opposite.

Tumbler cups

Tumbler cups are beaten from thick gauge silver with most of the weight in the base so that the cups return to an upright position when put on their

A Charles I beaker, printed initials 'T.G.', maker's mark 'HB'. 1641, 5in (12.5cm) high, 8.5oz, D

side. Because they are so solid they are almost impossible to damage. Most date from the late 17thC, but they were also made throughout the 18thC. Early ones tend to be short and very broad in relation to their height; later ones are taller and thinner.

Marks

Tumbler cups are usually marked in a group underneath the base or near the rim. Beakers were marked underneath the base until the end of the 18thC when they are marked in a line under the rim.

The broad, shallow shape of the beaker is typical of the period. Crests or coats of arms are engraved on more expensive ones.

By the 1750s tumbler cups were far narrower in relation to their height. Many surviving beakers and tumbler cups were made in provincial towns such as Newcastle and York.

A late 17thC Dutch miniature beaker, unmarked, with engraved foliate decoration, initialled 'RE'. c1700, 2.5in (6.5cm) high, 0.5oz, E

Beakers

*A George I tumbler cup, by
Richard Bailey of London, with
a gilt interior. 1719, 2.75in (7cm)
diam, E*

*A Russian beaker, assay master Ivan
Shagin, maker's mark unknown,
Moscow, with heart motifs. 1750, 3in
(7.5cm) high, 2.5oz, G*

*A George II tumbler cup, by Thomas
Cooke II & Richard Gurney of London,
with gilded bowl. c1754, 2.25in
(5.5cm) high, 1.5oz, G*

*A George III tumbler cup, by
Benjamin Brewood of London,
initialled 'RGL' below a crest. 1764,
3.25in (8cm) diam, G*

A Biedermeier tumbler and cover, by Wenzel Mayer of Vienna, decorated with a sculpted wolf, and chased with a hunting scene. 1840, 6in (15.5cm) high, 8oz, E

A pair of beakers, by William Marshall of Edinburgh, in the form of thistle heads, with gilt interiors. 1895, 2.5in (6.5cm) high, 3.5oz, H

A Guild of Handicraft beaker, by Charles Robert Ashbee, London, with spot-hammered decoration, with seven garnet cabochons. 1900, 5in (12.5cm) high, 5oz, C

A Guild of Handicraft Arts and Crafts beaker, Birmingham, with chased stylized decoration. 1901, 5in (12.5cm) high, 8oz, F

Tankards

A James II tankard, maker's mark 'RP' of London. 1685,
8.25in (21cm) high, 41.5oz, E

1. Does the tankard have a baluster-shaped body?
2. Is the lid domed?
3. Is the upper body marked in a line near the side of the handle or in a group underneath?
4. Does the inside of the lid have identical marks to those on the body, in a group?
5. Is the body quite plain, possibly with only a girdle for ornament?
6. Does the tankard have a rimmed foot?
7. Has the handle been hammered from sheet metal rather than cast?

Tankards

Although tankards dating from the reign of Charles I and the Commonwealth period have survived, the vast majority date from the end of the 17thC or later. Initially introduced for holding ale (a sweet sticky mead, quite unlike the beer of today), tankards were

A tankard, by John Seatoune of Edinburgh. 1702, 7.75in (19.5cm) high, 35.5oz, C

A tankard, by George Manjoy of London. 1692, 2.5in (6.5cm) high, 0.5oz, E

made in relatively large numbers. They remain among the most readily available pieces of 17thC silver, and continued to be used as drinking vessels until the late 18thC.

Marks

Tankards of the 17thC usually have four marks placed in a straight line by the handle; the same marks were also stamped on the lid. By the early 18thC marks on the lid were more usually found inside the vessel.

Plain shapes and simple decorative borders are characteristic of early tankards, such as the straight-sided version opposite, made in 1685.

Later tankards

By the end of the 18thC the use of tankards as drinking vessels had declined, largely because ale drinking had been replaced by wine drinking in fashionable circles. Tankards continued to be made after this into the Regency and Victorian periods, but these were produced in far smaller numbers and were made primarily as decorative or presentation pieces. Most of them are highly elaborate but shapes will still copy earlier styles.

Tankards

A silver tankard, by John Coney of Boston, MA, the flat lid with cast mask and dolphin thumbpiece and with engraved armorial. c1710, 7.25in (18.5cm) high, 32oz, C

A tankard, by Thomas Mason of London, embossed with later 19thC foliate decoration and a gentleman shooting. 1723, 7.5in (19cm) high, 28oz, F

A George II tankard, by Richard Bayley of London, the body with armorial engraving. 1729–30, 8in (20.5cm) high, 42oz, E

A tankard, by John Stuart of Providence, RI, the handle with whistle terminal, and engraved with 'W.T.F.'. c1735, 8in (20.5cm) high, 29oz, D

A tankard, by John Coburn of Boston, MA, the domed lid topped by a bell finial. c1755, 8.25in (21cm) high, 27oz, D

A tankard, by John Langlands I of Newcastle, the scroll handle with a heart terminal, marks rubbed. 1763, 8.25in (21cm) high, 34oz, E

An 18thC Russian tankard, unknown master 'A.E I' within a heart, Moscow mark, set with gold ten rouble coins. 1771, 6.25in (16cm) high, C

A tankard, by Nicholas Hearnden of London, decorated with a ribbed design. 1814, 6.75in (17cm) high, F

Mugs

A mug, by William Pearson of London. 1716,
4.75in (12cm) high, F

1. Is the mug marked in a group underneath?
2. Are the marks in pristine condition?
3. Is the crest or coat of arms original?
4. Does the mug stand on a separate foot?
5. Is the handle cast?
6. Is the body baluster-shaped?
7. Are there no splits in the rim?
8. Are the reinforcing patches at the handles original rather than a later addition?
9. Is there any damage to the sockets where the handle joins the body?

Mugs

The earliest mugs likely to be encountered date from the end of the 17thC and have slightly tapering cylindrical sides on a flat base. Late 17thC mugs include the 'thistle' shape, which originated in Scotland, but was also made in England. At this date, mugs have strap handles raised from sheet, and the bodies are generally plain, apart from a band of lobes and flutes, also found on late 17thC tankards. Other decoration such as chasing will almost certainly be an 18thC addition and is likely to include removal and replacement of the original arms or crest. The baluster-shaped mug was established in 1715, and usually has a cast handle. This shape predominated until the 1770s when straight-sided mugs were made with sheet handles – a change

An Irish mug, no maker's mark, Dublin. 1726, 4in (10cm) high, 7oz, G

perhaps assisted by the ready supply of sheet metal from the new rolling mills. Mugs, like tankards, ceased to be used for beer drinking in the late 18thC. Tankards are large and have lids; mugs are smaller and do not have lids and silversmiths found an alternative use for them as small presents. They were made for this purpose and were mostly smaller than before, throughout the 19thC, in a variety of styles.

Christening mugs

Many later more highly decorated mugs of the 19thC were made as christening presents, the finest of which came in cased sets with a knife, fork and spoon.

The mugs are usually of high quality and many have survived virtually unused. But the spoon has often been well used and may be badly worn.

A mug, by Timothy Ley of London. 1714, 4.25in (11cm) high, 8oz, E

Mugs

A baluster-shaped pint mug, unknown maker's mark 'JC' of Exeter and engraved beneath 'DD' over 'JY', the front later engraved with a crest. 1747, 5in (12.5cm) high, 12.5oz, G

A mug, by Pierre Amiraux of Jersey, scratched underneath with two sets of initials 'EBD' and 'EBT'. c1755, 4.75in (12cm) high, D

An early 19thC presentation mug, by Edward Lownes of Philadelphia, PA. 5.25in (13cm) high, 11.25oz, F

An embossed christening mug, by C. Reily & G. Storer of London, decorated with a Scottish archer and his companion. 1839, 4in (10cm) high, G

*An Indian colonial mug, by Hamilton
& Co. of Calcutta, with engraved foliate
decoration, on a foliate scroll foot, inscribed.
c1860, 5in (12.5cm) high, 7oz, H*

*A baluster mug, by George Unite of
Birmingham, embossed with an oval
reserve and floral swags under a husk band.
1870, 6.25in (16cm) high, 10.25oz, J*

*A christening mug, by Aldwinckle & Slater
of London, engraved with birds and animals
in Gothic arches, below wriggle work
decoration. 1887, 3.5in (9cm) high, 5oz, J*

*A Tiffany & Co. christening mug,
with engraved swags and boss
pattern, and 'Lisa 1946'. 1946,
3.25in (8cm) high, G*

Goblets

A wine cup, maker's mark 'FW' of London.
1630, 6.25in (16cm) high, 7oz, D

1. Is the goblet vase-shaped?
2. Does it have a stem foot?
3. Is there any engraved decoration?
4. Is the decoration bright-cut and in good, crisp condition?
5. Is it fully marked, probably underneath the base or on the rim foot?

Goblets

Goblets, or wine cups, which were made for secular use do not seem to pre-date Elizabethan times. With the onset of the Civil War very little silver was made and when Charles II returned he brought with him Continental fashions and new ideas. The novelty and availability of glass

A communion cup, by Robert Gardyne II of Dundee, engraved 'EX DONO IACOBI SMITH MERCATORIS'. c1640, 9in (23cm) high, 19.25oz, A

meant that silver cups for wine were forgotten about until reproductions were made in the 1770s.

The onset of Neo-classicism with its fondness for vase-shaped forms was entirely suited to the goblet, which remained in this style until the Regency period.

Collecting

Most 18thC goblets are vase-shaped but the standard and extent of decoration can vary considerably and this will alter the price.

Condition

The condition of goblets is important as many later examples have been subjected to very heavy use and may be damaged beyond repair. In particular, check for:
• splits in the bowl
• splits in the stem
• damage where bowl meets stem.

Vase-shaped goblets were made in large quantities throughout the 18thC and 19thC, and value therefore largely depends on the quality of the decoration and the reputation of the maker. The best examples are in silver gilt and have bright-cut engraving and a good coat of arms; the most ordinary pieces are plain and lightweight.

Later Regency goblets were of very high quality and tended to be made by the best makers of the time (e.g. Paul Storr for Rundell, Bridge & Rundell).

A goblet, by Robert & Samuel Hennell of London. 1810, 8in (20.5cm) high, F

Goblets

A late George III silver goblet, maker's mark '... A', London, with an embossed foliate band, a gadrooned base and on a circular foot. 1816, 5.5in (14cm) high, 258g (8.25oz) G

A pair of goblets, by William Barrett II of London, the campana bowls with embossed vine bands and acanthus leaves. 1819, 8.5in (21.5cm) high, 33.5oz, E

A goblet, by Robert Hennell III of London, the bowl embossed with a graduated design of teardrops on a scrolling ground. c1862, 7in (18cm) high, 12oz, G

A Gothic Revival chalice, by John Hardman & Co. of Birmingham, with applied panels of chased decoration and gem-set knopped stem, the base with religious symbols. 1869, 8in (20.5cm) high, 17oz, F

A late 19thC French goblet, by Jules Wiese with impressed Froment-Meurice mark, the stem formed as a lily mounted with a cherub riding a dolphin. 8.5in (21.5cm) high, 10.75oz, D

A German Historicism period lidded goblet, decorated with sculpted faces and hunting scenes, the socket lid with Cupid. c1880, 20in (51cm) high, 47oz, D

A Ramsden & Carr goblet, with an oviform bowl above a double foliate knop with wirework scroll embellishment. 1910, 5.75in (14.5cm) high, E

A set of four Artificers' Guild, goblets, the design attributed to Edward Spencer of London. 1923, 3.5in (9cm) diam, D

Tea and coffee services

Silver items associated with tea and coffee form a major collecting area. Apart from the pots themselves, there is a vast range of objects to choose from – from kettles and urns, sugar container and cream jugs, caddies and caddy spoons, to pairs of tongs and teaspoons, teapot stands and spoon trays. All of these have survived in England in substantially large numbers, but there are far fewer to be found in the United States. The earliest 18thC teapots were small because of the high cost of tea, which at this time was still a luxury commodity afforded by only the very rich. Many teapots have been badly damaged through frequent use. Check the pot for leaks and old repairs at spouts, handles, hinges and for any soldered joins. A good coat of arms is a great asset and the removal is noticeable because it is hard to get rid of the dent as it has to be done from inside. Although form changed over the years, decoration remained minimal, largely confined to a little engraving or flat chasing on the shoulder or bullet of Scottish teapots, and some attractive bright-cutting on late 18thC pots.

There is a curious gap in the middle of the 18thC when teapots do not seem to have been made in England at all, although they continued to be produced in Scotland. During this gap in production of teapots a number of tea kettles were produced, and later, in the 1760s, these were replaced by tea urns. Tea kettles were obviously expensive due to their size and complexity and the fact that, apart from the earliest examples, they were profusely decorated with flat chasing. Most kettles had a salver-like stand which between c1730 and 1750 was occasionally triangular in shape. These rarely survive with the kettle today but are occasionally offered for sale on their own as trays or waiters. Although tea urns were made earlier in the 18thC, it was not until the 1760s that they became popular. Some had burners, but most had a heated iron bar that fitted into a container inside the body, providing a much cleaner way of heating the water than using a flame. Urns were made in a wide variety of designs but the basic form was always vase- or ovoid-shaped. Although urns and kettles are decorative they are large and take up a lot of space and they are not popular with collectors. As with any silver that has been subjected to a direct source of heat, always check carefully for wear; often the marks on the base will have been erased.

This example (right) by the famous silversmiths Emes & Barnard is typical in style of the beginning of the Regency period. It has a long inscription to a deceased former employee and the crest and motto of the Edinburgh Friendly Insurance Society. Although the makers are considered highly collectable, such inscriptions will tend to make the piece less saleable.

Like teapots, coffee pots are largely plain, although a few early examples were engraved with cut-card decoration and some very elaborate Rococo pots were produced towards the middle of the 18thC. Both octagonal teapots and coffee pots

A George III tea urn, by Emes & Barnard of London. 1811, 13in (33cm) high, 112oz, E

made at the beginning of the 18thC are particularly sought after and because they are rare they command high prices. Early coffee pots had raised rather than cast spouts, sometimes with a hinged flap, and sometimes placed at right angles to the handle. Coffee pots were straight-sided until the 1730s when the bellied body with a tuck-in foot appeared, only to be replaced with the vase shape in the 1760s when there was a Classical revival. Some elaborate Regency coffee pots have stands and burners. Chocolate pots were only made up until c1730. Virtually identical to coffee pots, they had a hinged or detachable cap or finial in the lid. Through this, a rod was inserted to stir up the chocolate sediment. A knowledge of the shapes of both coffee and teapots provides a useful aid to dating, but it is important to remember that many 18thC styles were repeated in the 19thC and 20thC, so always check the marks. Although there is nothing wrong with a reproduction, they are worth considerably less than an original. Tea and coffee services from before the 1790s are rare, and most date from the Victorian times when they were made in an infinite variety, usually very elaborate, and sometimes in fitted wooden chests,

A provincial George I teapot, by John Carnaby of Newcastle. 1721, 6.25in (16cm) high, 11.5oz, E

occasionally complete with matching trays. Because services are available in large numbers and in such a variety of combinations, they are popular among collectors today.

Tea caddies were often expensive and elaborate, again reflecting the high price of tea. Finely engraved coats of arms feature prominently on early oblong caddies and the quality of decoration on mid-18thC examples can be very high. From the 1730s caddies are found in pairs with a

134

matching sugar container and some were made to fit into a lockable case. It is interesting to note that caddies themselves acquired locks in the 1760s when tea was no longer such an expensive commodity as it had been earlier on in the century. Although most caddies date from the 18thC a number of small reproductions were made around the beginning of the 20thC; however, these are less collectable today.

Early 18thC sugar containers are rare. Most date from the end of the century and the combination of Classical shape and attractive engraving makes them very collectable. Cream or milk jugs were produced in the 18thC in a variety of shapes and sizes; early examples had small spouts and were probably used for milk, but from the 1720s onwards jugs with a broader lip, more suitable for cream, were made. One of the more unusual and amusing variations of the cream jug is the cow creamer, made in the 18thC mainly by John Schuppe.

A Tiffany & Co. five-piece tea service, with floral repoussé decoration.
11.25in (29cm) high, 95.5oz, E

Teapots

*An apple-shaped teapot, by Colin MacKenzie of
Edinburgh, assay master Edward Penman. 1721,
6in (15.5cm) high, 20.5oz, C*

1. Is it pear-shaped?
2. Does it have a wooden handle and finial?
3. Is the body marked in a line underneath?
4. Is the cover marked with the maker's mark and lion's head erased?
5. Is the hinge on the lid secure?
6. Are the seams free from damage?
7. Is the cover domed?

Early teapots

Early teapots date from the reign of Queen Anne. Tea had only begun to be drunk in quantities at the turn of the 18thC. It was very expensive and this is reflected in the small size of many early teapots. Shapes changed quite considerably, from pear-shaped in the early 18thC to bullet-shaped mid-century, and later drum-shaped. Octagonal teapots were only made for a very short time (c1710–25) and are very rare and expensive today. Early pots had wooden handles and finials; these were replaced with ivory during the Regency period and silver in the 19thC. Scottish teapots also tend to have silver handles.

Bullet teapots

Bullet-shaped teapots were made from c1730–45 and are relatively rare today. Some bullet teapots have no side seam; these examples were raised in one piece and the base was put on after the hinge had been fitted

to the inside and the lid had been attached. This type nearly always has a loose lid after 250 years of wear and therefore it is virtually impossible to repair the hinge properly.

Decoration

The best-quality bullet-shaped teapots are finely engraved around the shoulder and have a fine coat of

An octagonal teapot, by Richard Green of London. 1718, 6in (15.5cm) high, 17.5oz, C

arms. Less expensive ones will be plain. Early Queen Anne teapots are usually plain, but some fine examples by Huguenot makers are embellished with cut-card work. Much George I domestic silver is unadorned, although in the 1730s bullet teapots were often engraved at the shoulders and corner of the lid with bands of masks and strapwork.

A bullet-shaped teapot, maker's mark 'HC' of London. 1694, 4.25in (11cm) high, 11oz, E

Teapots

A 'lighthouse-form' teapot, by Jacob Marius Groen of New York, with 'Onslow' thumb tab. c1730, 9.5in (24cm) high, 31.5oz, D

A tapered-vase-form teapot, by Milne & Campbell of Glasgow, with swan-neck spout and decorated with acanthus garlands. c1765, 9in (23cm) high, 25oz, F

A pear-form teapot, possibly by John Swift of London, embossed with floral sprays and later eagle and motto crests, with eagle-head spout and finial. 1774, G

A cylindrical bright-cut teapot and stand, by John Lloyd of Dublin. 1778, teapot 10in (25.5cm) wide, stand 5.5in (14cm) diam, 21oz, F

A shaped oval-form teapot, by Peter & Jonathan Bateman of London, with bright-cut decoration and flush hinged, domed cover. 1790, 11in (28cm) long, 12oz, E

A circular fluted shaped teapot, by Thomas Holland II of London, with reeded girdle below a hinged cover and with ebonized fluted finial and loop handle. 1805, 6in (15.5cm) diam, 15.75oz, G

A teapot, by Harvey Lewis of Philadelphia, PA, the base inscribed 'J. Tatnall to S. Lea 5 Mo. 28th 1813'. c1813, 7.5in (19cm) high, 18.25oz, G

A teapot, by James Stamp of Dublin, embossed with a band of Vitruvian scrolls. 1817, 6.25in (16cm) high, 28oz, G

Teapots

*A teapot, by Thomas Fletcher &
Sidney Gardiner of Philadelphia,
PA. 1815–30, 10.5in (26.5cm) wide,
52oz, F*

*A coin silver teapot, by Bailey
& Kitchen of Philadelphia, PA.
c1835, 12in (30.5cm) high,
46.5oz, G*

*A compressed melon-shaped teapot, by Paul
Storr for Storr & Mortimer, London, flat
chased to the shoulder and lid with a band of
anthemion and scrolls. 1836, 4.5in (11.5cm)
high, 23oz, G*

*A Scottish teapot with burner,
maker's mark 'CR & S', of
Edinburgh, with moulded
blossoms and rocailles. 1857–8,
13in (33cm) high, 48oz, E*

A teapot from a picnic service, designed by Christopher Dresser, produced by Hukin & Middleton, London. c1879, 3.5in (9cm) high, H

A Birmingham Guild of Handicraft teapot, by Arthur Stansfield Dixon, set with malachite finial and ebonized wood handle. 1899, 6in (15.5cm) high, G

A Fabergé teapot, of plain ovoid form with a stippled ground, with a scroll handle and turned ivory knop. 1896–1908, 6in (15.5cm) high, E

An Art Deco teapot, by Goldsmiths & Silversmiths Co. of London, on a raised circular foot with geometric decoration. 1932, 10in (25.5cm) long, 22oz, H

Coffee pots

An octagonal coffee pot, by Thomas Folkingham of London. 1711, 9.25in (23.5cm) high, 30oz, D

1. Are the hallmarks in a line to the right of the handle, or scattered under the foot?
2. Is the lid also marked, with only the lion passant and maker's mark? (Duty mark added after 1784.)
3. Is there a contemporary coat of arms on the body?
4. Are the proportions of the pot in keeping with its date? (Odd proportions may indicate the pot is a conversion from a tankard.)
5. If the pot was made in England, does it have a wooden handle? (Silver, ivory or composition handles are usually later replacements and reduce value.)
6. Does the inside of the pot have a dull appearance? (A polished finish could indicate it has been altered in some way.)
7. Is any decoration flat chased?

Coffee pots

Most coffee and chocolate pots date from c1700 onwards when these beverages became popular, although examples of earlier ones do exist. They are usually much the same size, but some considerably smaller pots by good makers were produced in the 1700s, which are expensive for their size today. Queen Anne pots are of plain form, enlivened only by a coat of arms or cut-card decoration. Early lids are domed, becoming flat

A straight tapering coffee pot, by Peter Archambo I, London. 1729, 9in (23cm) high, 28.5oz, D

by the 1730s and thereafter rising again until the end of the century. The earliest coffee pots, such as the one shown oposite, had highly domed lids; handles were often placed at right angles to the spout and the body

was unadorned. A hinged spout flap and decoration on the lid will add to the value. Coffee pots are extremely popular with collectors and good ones fetch high prices.

Decoration

Decoration became more varied during the 18thC. Flat-chased bands around the top and bottom of a pot were typical embellishments in the 1740s, as were asymmetric cartouches and tuck-in feet. Irish coffee pots were often covered in chased decoration. In England, however, all-over shell and flower scroll decoration did not become prevalent until the Victorian period.

Armorials

A coat of arms or monogram would often be placed opposite the handle, so that guests would be able to see them when the pot was being used.

A coffee pot, by Charles Lemaitre of Dublin. c1733, 9.5in (24cm) high, D

143

Coffee pots

An early 18thC Maltese baluster coffee jug, possibly by Michele Pianta, Vilhena period, the body with part-chasing and part-embossing. 5in (20.5cm) high, 12oz, D

A flared-form coffee pot, by Ebenezer Oliphant of Edinburgh, assay master Dougal Ged, with chased borders of flower head, fruit and scroll decoration. 1741, 11in (28cm) high, 30oz, D

A plain pear-shaped coffee jug, possibly by Thomas Jeanes of London, with acanthus-capped elongated lip, the domed egg-and-dart cover with spire finial. 1767, 9.5in (24cm) high, 17oz, F

A baluster coffee pot, by William Grundy of London, embossed with flowering foliage, the ogee domed cover with a twist lobed finial. 1770, 10.5in (26.5cm) high, 30.5oz, F

A coffee pot, by Joseph & Nathaniel Richardson of Philadelphia, PA, with engraved monogram for Mordecai and Hannah Lewis. c1780, 12.5in (32cm) high, 34.25oz, B

An Empire-style coffee pot, by Amable Brasier of Philadelphia, PA, with milled floral decoration and spreading foot. 1810–30, 11.25in (28.5cm) high, E

A coffee pot, by Robert Garrard of London, with swan-necked fluted spout, resting on a simple foot rim chased with foliate and shell borders. 1825, 9in (23cm) high, 27oz, G

An Italian coffee pot, the tubular spout with animal terminal, hallmarked for Genoa. c1830, 11in (28cm) high, 27oz, G

Coffee pots

*A baluster-form coffee pot, by
Charles Fox of London, chased with
scrollwork, shells and foliage. 1833,
11in (28cm) high, 35oz, G*

*A lobed baluster coffee pot, by John
Wrangham & William Moulson of London,
with an apple and leaf finial, engraved with a
crest. 1838, 9.75in (25cm) high, 32.25oz, G*

*A crested coffee pot, by R. & S.
Garrard of London, engraved with a
crest, garter motto and badge of the
Order of the Bath. 1841, 9.5in (24cm)
high, 34oz, F*

*A Swiss ovoid pedestal coffee pot, by Rehfuss
& Cie of Bern, with a lion finial, the handle
terminating with a ram's head, the spout
with a lion's head. c1840, 10.5in (26.5cm)
high, 26.5oz, G*

A Victorian oval and straight tapering coffee pot, by Samuel Smily of London, with an ivory double scroll handle and pineapple finial. 9.25in (23.5cm) high, 27.5oz, H

A coffee pot stand and burner, by W. & J. Barnard of London, the coffee pot of bellied circular outline with fluted upper section. 1891, 9.5in (24cm) high, 42oz, G

An embossed tapering-form coffee pot, by Walter & Charles Sissons of London. 1905, 9in (23cm) high, 16oz, H

An Art Deco coffee pot, by the International Silver Company, New England. c1925, 8.75in (22cm) high, J

Tea and coffee services

A four-piece tea service, by William Burwash & Richard Sibley of London, with part-fluted, circular bodies and gadrooned borders. 1812, 97oz, E

1. Is the set heavy?
2. Are all the pieces identically marked?
3. Are all the detachable pieces – lids, bases, burner – all part-marked to match?
4. Does the design correspond to the period?
5. Is the fluting free from damage? (Splits or lead solder repairs.)
6. Is the body thin where a coat of arms has been removed?
7. Are the hinges tight?

Tea services

Although matching tea items were made at the beginning of the 18thC the idea of a tea service did not become popular until c1790. Designs tended to follow the fashions of silver of the time, therefore tea services were elegant and bright-cut in the 1790s, solid and richly decorated in the Regency period and mass-produced with an abundance of lavish decoration during the reign of Queen Victoria.

Condition

A teapot is the most used part of a set. Subsequently its state of wear will be a good guide to the overall condition of the set. Make sure to check for damage to the feet, which are particularly fragile, and for repairs to the body with lead solder, which may be hidden in the chasing.

A four-piece tea and coffee set, by John & Joseph Angell of London. 1832, coffee pot 11in (28cm) high, 94oz, E

Victorian eagle finials often get damaged and as the pattern was also made in plate, a silver pot may have a plated finial.

Several features add to desirability:
• elegant shape
• matching coats of arms on all of the pieces
• bright-cutting in good condition.

Victorian and later tea services

Most tea services that come on the market today are from the Victorian period or later.

Make sure that every item in the set is marked with the same date and maker. Later tea services will sometimes come complete with matching large trays.

A five-piece tea and coffee service, by Chaudron & Rasch of Philadelphia, PA, of shaped rectangular form, decorated with pressed strap work and gadrooned borders. c1812, tallest 10.25in (26cm) high, 137oz, D

Tea and coffee services

A six-piece tea service, by Edward Lownes of Philadelphia, PA, the lids with bird and nest finial, gadrooned borders, grapevine and leafage at shoulders and serpent spout and handles. c1825, 178oz, E

A four-piece tea set, by John Samuel Hunt of London, retailed by Hunt & Roskell, late Storr & Mortimer, chased with a foliate and mask border. 1861, 71oz, F

A four-piece Rococo Revival tea service, by Elkington & Co. Ltd of Birmingham, of pedestal form repoussé with scrolls and flowers. 1893, coffee pot 10.75in (27.5cm) high, 92oz, F

An early 20thC Chinese export three-piece tea service, with bamboo form handles and spouts, decorated with Chinese floral and figural scenes. Teapot 5.25in (13cm) high, 29oz, E

A six-part tea and coffee set, by EBS Ltd of London, retail stamp for Gebrüder Friedländer. 1913, hot water pot 12in (30.5cm) high, 237oz, D

A German Theodor Müller no 5475 hammered four-part tea and coffee service, with ivory handles and finials. c1920, coffee pot 10in (25.5cm) high, E

A five-piece tea service, by Albert Edward Jones of Birmingham. 1928–30, coffee pot 7.5in (19cm) high, D

A 1930s Puiforcat five-piece silver coffee and tea set. The half-reeded canisters with applied silver bead, hardwood covers and 'C'-form handles, show the clean lines of Art Deco. Coffee pot 5.5in (14cm) high, D

Jugs

A hot water jug, by Emick
Romer of London. 1767,
10.5in (26.5cm) high,
20oz, F

1. Is the body baluster-shaped?
2. Does it have a lid?
3. Does it have a central foot?
4. Is there a contemporary coat of arms?
5. Is the handle cast?
6. Is the patina suitably aged?
7. Are there any dents to the central belly?
8. Does the jug feel heavy and solid?

Jugs

Large jugs intended for beer or wine came into use with the restoration of Charles II. Some of the early ones have covers, but after the 1730s these are very rare. They do not have insulated handles and were probably never designed to hold anything hot; if a jug has an ivory handle this will have been added later. Most 18thC jugs are baluster-shaped and, up until the reign of George II, had plain bodies. Following this, Rococo influences would lead to more elaborate designs.

A mid-18thC Venetian Republic coffee jug, maker's mark 'ZM'. 9.5in (24cm) high, 15.5oz, F

Collecting

Unlike tankards, which were made in large quantities, beer jugs were far more important pieces of silver and designed to be used in only the grandest of homes. Consequently, they are far rarer and more expensive today. A good coat of arms is a welcome feature on a jug and some of the best examples have cut-card decoration to the lip. The jug below by Charles Wright is typical of this restrained Classical decoration.

Marks

Most jugs have a full set of marks on the base, or on the body to one side of the handle near the rim. Early cover marking is erratic.

Shaving jugs

Shaving jugs are very rare, made only during the reigns of George I and Queen Anne. They always have a cover, but they are smaller than beer jugs and are oval in shape. Originally they were accompanied by a large oval basin with a cut-out in the border, designed to hold under the chin, but the two parts are frequently separated and the jug sold on its own.

A hot water jug, by Charles Wright of London. 1773, 11in (28cm) high, 24oz, F

Jugs

An 'ascos' ewer, by Paul Storr of London. The ascos jug follows an ancient Greek prototype used as a receptacle for the oil burnt in lamps. 1835, 8.75in (22cm) high, 32oz, D

A hot water jug, by J. McKay of Edinburgh, engraved with flora and scrolls. 1858, 13.75in (35cm) high, 33.75oz, F

A hot water jug, by Nichols & Plinke of St Petersburg, the neck repoussé with serrated semi-gadroon, the body with guilloché and semi-gadrooned ornament. c1866–70, 11in (28cm) high, 38oz, E

A wine jug, by Gorham Mfg Co. of Providence, RI, decorated with repoussé Bacchanalian motifs. c1875, 14.25in (36cm) high, 80oz, C

*A Tiffany & Co. water jug,
with hand-hammered
finish and applied handle.
1877, 7.75in (19.5cm) high,
27oz, D*

*An Aesthetic Movement Tiffany & Co. jug,
with hammered surface, decorated as a
pool with three copper carp and two copper
and brass dragonflies above. c1880, 7.25in
(18.5cm) high, 27oz, A*

*A jug, by Heinrich Vogeler, made
by Wilkens & Sons, designed to
accompany the cutlery series
'Meadow Saffron'. c1902, 8.25in
(21cm) high, E*

*An Omar Ramsden
hot water jug,
London. 1921,
7.75in (19.5cm)
high, 17.25oz, D*

Tea urns

*An inverted pear-form tea urn, by Thomas Whipham &
Charles Wright of London. 1767, 20in (52.5cm) high,
101oz, E*

1. Is it fully marked either underneath (if Georgian) or on the body
   (if Victorian)?
2. Is the cover part-marked with the maker's mark, lion passant and
   sovereign's head?
3. Is there any evidence of the internal fittings having been removed?
4. Is there any sign of any visible repairs? (Taps and spouts are
   especially vulnerable.)
5. If the base is separate has it been marked?
6. Does the tap work? (Although this is desirable, it is not essential.)

Tea urns

Tea urns were made from the 1760s onwards, and were probably used for holding hot water to replenish the pot rather than for tea itself. Although a few urns have burners, most, especially plated examples, have a cylindrical inner sleeve to hold a hot iron bar, which proved to be just as effective as a burner. Sizes and shapes vary greatly and there is no such thing as a 'typical' tea urn. Despite their variety and decorative qualities, urns are not especially popular with collectors and they remain relatively inexpensive today. Initially, urns had charcoal burners, internal hollow flues that heated the water and no internal fittings. Always check any openwork for any cracks

A circular tea urn, by John Emes of London. 1807, 15in (38cm) high, 141oz, E

and damage caused by the heat. Regency tea urns of this type are particularly expensive.

The circular tea urn below left made by John Emes in 1807 has a stand integral to the body. The lion's head handles are typical.

Tea kettles

Tea kettles made for boiling water at the table date from the 1730s. They comprise two or three parts – kettle, stand and a burner, which is sometimes separate. These are much smaller than tea urns and usually have a lower capacity and weigh considerably less.

Early examples are circular and will be relatively plain in form.

Reproductions

Tea kettles waned in popularity after c1760 although they reappeared in the mid-Victorian period as part of tea sets.

An Arts and Crafts tea urn, by Omar Ramsden & Alwyn Carr. c1908, 12.5in (32cm) high, E

Tea caddies

A pair of tea caddies and a sugar box, by William Plummer of London. 1767, caddies 5.75in (14.5cm) high, 39oz, D

1. Is there a full set of hallmarks on the base of each of the caddies?
2. Is the cover of each caddy marked with the maker's mark and lion passant?
3. Are the coat of arms contemporary to the piece?
4. Is there any damage to the feet?
5. Are the finials intact?
6. Is the tortoiseshell veneer complete on the case?
7. Do the caddies fit into the case properly?
8. Does any crest or coat of arms on the case match that on the caddies?

Early caddies

The earliest caddies date from the reign of Queen Anne. Early caddies are oblong or oval with a sliding base and a detachable lid, which was used as a measure for the tea. By about 1780 the cap measure was replaced by the caddy spoon.

Later caddies

Initially, caddies came in pairs for the two types of tea available – Black and Green – but by the middle of the 18thC they were made with a bowl, initially thought to be for mixing the tea but now generally believed to be for holding sugar.

At the end of the 18thC caddies had locks, although this is surprising as by this time tea was no longer as expensive as earlier in the century.

A oval-form tea caddy, by Duncan Urquhart & Naphtali Hart of London. c1802, 6.75in (17cm) high, 14.25oz, E

By the late 18thC caddies were much larger and were made singly; sometimes they would have an internal dividing sheet so that they could hold two different types of tea. Pairs will always be more desirable than singles.

Rococo-style caddies

The fine set of three 1767 caddies and sugar box pictured opposite shows the silversmith taking full advantage of the Rococo Revival style.

Chasing

Chased decoration tends to be less popular on silver than a good plain surface and will only add to the value if it is in very good condition.

Scottish tea caddies

Scottish tea caddies from before the reign of George IV are very rare.

A tea caddy, maker's mark overstruck, 'T', of London. 1779, 4in (10cm) high, 13oz, E

Tea caddies

A George III tea caddy, maker's mark 'IL' of London, with armorial engraving. 1783–4, 5in (12.5cm) high, 19oz, E

A tea caddy, by Crispin Fuller of London, with part-fluted decoration and urn finial. 1796, 7in (18cm) high, 15oz, F

A tea caddy, by Reily & Storer of London, of serpentine bombé form, with floral finial to the chinoiserie-decorated cover, all within a 'C'-scroll and floral cartouche. 1851–2, 5.25in (13cm) high, 14oz, F

A tea caddy, by William Stocker of London, shaped oval form, bright-cut decoration, flush hinged cover with an ivory finial, engraved with a crest. 1861, 5in (12.5cm) long, 11oz, G

A tea canister, by Whiting Mfg Co., New York, with spot-hammered decoration, applied with copper and silver maple leaves. c1880, 4in (10cm) high, 9oz, F

A late 19thC Japanese tea caddy, decorated with a sinuous dragon in high relief. 5.75in (14.5cm) high, 9oz, E

A tea caddy, by Charles Stuart Harris of London, with chinoiserie and Rococo figures in foliate-scroll settings, with a figural finial. 1896, 5in (12.5cm) high, 16oz, G

A Liberty & Co. 'Cymric' tea caddy and matching spoon, by Archibald Knox, the cover with Celtic scroll border enamelled in shades of green and yellow, Birmingham. 1903, 6in (15.5cm) high, D

Sugar bowls and baskets

*A George III navette pedestal sugar basket, by Henry
Chawner of London. 1789, 6.25in (16cm) long, 6.75oz, H*

1. Is the bowl or basket fully marked?
2. Is the handle or cover also marked?
3. Is any coat of arms or crest on the body original?
4. Does it have a central foot?
5. Are the handle joints free from damage?
6. Are the handles unbroken?
7. If a basket, does it measure about 6in (15.5cm) in length?

Development of styles

Sugar was originally kept in silver sugar boxes, which first appeared at the end of the 17thC and continued into the reign of Queen Anne. As much of the sugar was cultivated in the West Indies, it is not surprising that a number of these boxes appear in the United States. By the beginning of the 18thC sugar was kept in silver bowls, with covers.

A George I sugar bowl and cover, by John Gibbons of London. 1724, 4.5in (11.5cm) diam, 6.5oz, E

By the middle of the 18thC the covers developed cone finials and thereafter the bodies became vase-shaped with covers that were sometimes cut to hold spoons. In the 1770s the bowls were eventually replaced by larger, open sugar baskets, before being made as part of tea sets.

The basket in the main picture opposite is most frequently sold either as a sugar or sweetmeat basket. Sometimes these later baskets are fitted with a glass liner.

The early sugar bowl below left, made by John Gibbons in 1724, is typically plain, although some examples do have a crest or coat of arms. Check that the marks on the cover match those on the bowl.

Sugar vase

The sugar vase below represents the final development of the sugar bowl with a cover. The example by maker 'CM' in 1746 would have been made as part of a set with two caddies. These vases are generally good quality. This one is decorated with drapery, but leaves, and shells are also popular.

Irish sugar bowls

Quite a large number of Irish sugar bowls appear on the market, made in either Dublin or Cork. Irish provincial silver always commands a premium and it is much sought after by collectors.

A sugar vase, maker's mark 'CM', London. 1773, 8in (20.5cm) high, 9oz, G

Sugar bowls

A George II sugar bowl, by Archibald Ure of Edinburgh, with family crest. 1731, 4.75in (12cm) diam, 5.5oz, F

A George III sugar basket, by William Plummer of London, the wirework with a wavy rim, the sides with applied foliage and medallions, crested. 1772, 3.5in (9cm) high, 3oz, H

A pair of George III graduated sugar bowls, by William Stroud of London, the lower sections with stiff leaves, on hoof feet, engraved with an armorial. 1796, tallest 4.75in (12cm) high, 20oz, F

A German sugar bowl and cover, the foot on four cast paw feet rising to a pierced openwork bowl depicting Classical figures and rinceau with winged caryatid handles, with blue glass liner. c1809–19, 8in (20.5cm) high, 19oz, G

A sugar basket, by D. C. Hands of London, with a vine leaf and grape handle, the basket with pierced and reticulated sides with game birds in tree branches. 1853–4, 7in (18cm) high, 8oz, G

A novelty sugar vase and cover, modelled as a standing owl, by George Richards & Edward Brown of London, with textured feathers, with red and black glass eyes, on a raised foot with foliate decoration. 1866, 9in (23cm) high, 21oz, D

A Britannia standard sugar caster, by William Comyns & Sons Ltd of London, with a pierced and fruit-and leaf-embossed cover, with three asymmetric shoulder handles. 1896, 7.25in (18.5cm) high, 13oz, H

An Edwardian sugar basket, by John Henry Rawlings of London, the pierced body with swag and bow decoration and floral detailed swing handle, with matched sifter spoon. 1909, G

Cream jugs

A George II cream jug, by Louis Cuny of London. 1731, 5in
(12.5cm) high, 5oz, F

1. Is it fully marked in a group underneath?
2. Does the body stand on a rim foot?
3. Is the form simple?
4. Is there any decoration on the body?
5. Does it feel solid to hold?
6. Are there any join lines visible on the inside? (If so, the jug has been cast.)

Milk and cream jugs

Milk jugs were first made in the early years of the 18thC. Those made during the reign of Queen Anne followed the lines of teapots of the period. From c1720 onwards milk or cream was served cold and jugs became smaller and silver replaced wood as the material for handles.

By the end of the 18thC milk and cream jugs were usually made as part of tea sets, generally by the same makers who produced teapots. The George II cream jug illustrated in the main picture opposite is a good-quality early 18thC example. Some early 18thC cream jugs have cast bodies and on these the join lines are sometimes visible down the inside of the body.

Marks

Milk and cream jugs are marked either on their side or underneath.

A George II provincial squat baluster cream jug, by Pentecost Symonds of Plymouth, Exeter. 1748, 2.25in (5.5cm) high, 2.5oz, G

Beware

Conversions of less desirable or useful pieces of silver into practical and collectable milk and cream jugs abound. Not all of these are intended to deceive people but among

A George II helmet cream jug, by Robert Innes of London. 1752, 4in (10cm) high, 5.5oz, G

the wares most commonly converted into milk jugs are pepper casters and christening mugs. Helmet cream jugs, such as this one above, made by Robert Innes of London in 1752, are also highly desirable and are worth substantially more than plain baluster-shaped examples of the same date. The high quality of this jug is reflected in the well-moulded spout and the wire-reinforced rim, which also add to its durability.

Cream jugs

A George III silver baluster cream jug, by Thomas Shepherd of London, embossed with pastoral scenes and a swimming swan, below a punch-beaded rim. 1778, 4.5in (11.5cm) high, 3.5oz, H

A George III cream pail, by George Gray of London, of wirework form embossed with animals, birds and buildings, with beaded borders, on three pierced bracket feet. 1778, 3.25in (8cm) high, 2oz, G

A George III cream jug, by Benjamin Mordecai (alias Benjamin Mountigue) of London, the barrel-shaped body with reeded bands. 1785, 4in (10cm) high, 6.5oz, H

A George III vase-shaped cream jug, by John Bull of London, with a beaded border and engraved with leaves, bands and a cartouche. 1790, 5.5in (14cm) high, 3.25oz, H

A George III Irish provincial cream jug, by Carden Terry & John Williams of Cork, with part-fluted decoration below drapes and foliate decoration. c1810, 5in (12.5cm) high, 5oz, F

A lobed-baluster cream jug, by John Wakefield of London, with leaf-capped scroll handle. 1830, 7in (18cm) high, 8oz, H

A cream jug, by Ramsden & Carr of London, mounted to the handle with a turquoise enamel cabochon. 1904, 5.5in (14cm) long, E

A early 20thC Tiffany & Co. silver-mounted nautilus shell jug, in Renaissance revival style, the scrolling handle to a concave-sided pedestal foot. 6in (15.5cm) high, G

Wine

Since the 1760s wine has been an increasingly popular drink in Britain and consequently most silver items associated with the wine trade have been produced in large quantities and are quite readily available today. Associated items include claret jugs, wine coolers, wine coasters for holding the glass decanters, wine funnels for decanting and silver wine labels for wine bottles. Although glass was used for drinking vessels since the earliest times, the 19thC saw the development of the silver or silver-mounted claret jug. Due to the increased popularity of drinking wine, silversmiths began improving glass decanters used in the 18thC by adding bands of silver and replacing glass stoppers with silver-hinged lids. In the second quarter of the century, silver handles and larger mounts were added.

From the middle of the century, claret jugs became one of the favoured items for silversmiths to display their skill. Sometimes this would produce classical examples such as this claret jug by Stephen Smith, opposite, or in some cases the silversmith would look further back to ancient history for inspiration, such as the ewer on p173. Here the famous silversmith Paul Storr has taken inspiration from Ancient Greek and Etruscan 'oinochoe' or wine jugs. These items inspired by ancient civilizations were particularly desired by the wealthy minority who embarked on the European Grand Tour. Claret jugs were produced throughout Europe, including collectable French examples. Other exceptional examples, which are highly collectable, are those made by the Russian firms of Gratchev or Fabergé. From the 1850s, many of the leading British manufacturers were producing fabulous hand-engraved glass bodies. The majority of their silver mounts were hallmarked in Birmingham and Sheffield. By the third quarter of the century, jugs of the most bizarre form were in great fashion, closely followed by those inspired by the Aesthetic and Art Nouveau movements.

Wine coolers mostly date from the second half of the 18thC, but a number were produced before the 1770s. They were made in pairs and are surprisingly plentiful for such expensive objects. Most are based on the vase or bucket shape, but some were made in imitation of the Warwick vase. Classical motifs feature strongly on the massive Regency coolers of Rundell, Bridge & Rundell, whereas Victorian coolers revert to more naturalistic decoration. A number of Sheffield plate wine coolers are sold without their lids and collars, and although these are worth considerably less than a complete silver example, they make attractive flower vases.

Wine coasters were made in huge numbers from the reign of George II onwards. Most of them have wooden bases, sometimes with a crested silver disc; more expensive variations have silver bottoms, which should be separately marked. Some are very expensive and heavy silver gilt coasters were made in Regency times with the sides cast in sections. A number of novelty silver wine vessels are of interest to the collector. The need for passing two bottles round a table at the same time (presumably Port and Madeira) led to the 18thC introduction of the 'jolly boat', an open double stand on four small casters, and the decanter trolley, basically a pair of coasters

A claret jug, by Stephen Smith of London, profusely chased with floral swags, the cover cast with a finial of a rearing fox. 1865, F

joined by a wheeled chassis with a handle at the front. Coasters for holding decanters continued to be produced throughout the 19thC, which suggests the two vessels were used together. Solid-bodied examples were followed a little later by glass jugs with silver mounts. These are popular as they can look very decorative on a table. Plain glass bodies are not as popular as frosted or engraved examples, and in general the more elaborate the glass the higher the quality of the mounts. Particularly sought-after jugs include some made in the 1880s with 'rock crystal' bodies and the 'Cellini' and the 'Armada' jugs, both of which are very decorative. When buying such items check that all the individual pieces are marked. Wine was decanted through a silver funnel. These are nearly always plain, with only a decorative border for variety.

Although the rare early 18thC examples have straight spouts, later ones have the spout turned to the side to allow the wine to trickle down the side of the decanter. Many spouts have been trimmed straight, affecting the value.

18thC wine bottles did not have paper labels and the need to know the contents of the bottle after it had been removed from the bin led to the introduction of the silver wine label in the 1740s. This is one of the few collecting areas where the earliest examples are by no means the most expensive.

A George IV Scottish provincial wine label, by William Ferguson of Peterhead, with Edinburgh marks, incised and blackened 'MADEIRA'. 1826, 1.75in (4.5cm) wide, F

Prices depend far more on the subject and the decoration. Popular titles such as Port, Brandy, Sherry and Claret are more readily saleable because unlike obscure names they can be used on present-day decanters. Gin is sometimes spelt backwards as 'Nig', perhaps to confuse the servants or to gloss over the drinking of such a common tipple! Labels are generally hung from a chain; others are suspended from a wire hoop, which slips over the neck of the bottle, but the presence of chain or hoop makes little difference to value as modern replacements can be easily made. Smaller silver labels were also produced in large numbers for sauce bottles.

Some collectors concentrate on the great variety of designs, others on the multiplicity of names on labels, on the silversmiths and other makers, or on the place of manufacture. The George IV Scottish provincial wine label opposite, by William Ferguson of Peterhead has a rather common name 'Madeira', but the interest and value are increased due to its designer, the fact that it is provincial and because it also has assay marks for Edinburgh. This pushes its value over £1,000, whereas many 'Madeira'

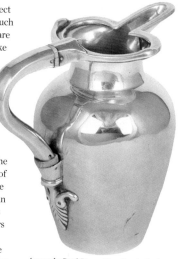

A ewer, by Paul Storr of London, in the form of a 5thC Etruscan bronze oinochoe. 1798, 6.75in (17cm) high, 20oz, E

labels can be found for £100–200. English wine tasters of the type with a domed centre are very rare. However, small two-handled dishes were made in large numbers in the second half of the 17thC that are frequently described as tasters but which could have equally well been sweetmeat dishes. One small dish is the earliest known piece of American silver.

Claret jugs

A mounted glass claret jug, by 'IF' of London, the mounts cast with Bacchanalian masks and vines. c1875, 11.25in (28.5cm) high, F

1. Is the body fully marked and the cover part-marked?
2. If the foot is silver-mounted does it, too, bear marks?
3. Is the glass original, and almost certainly decorated in some way? (Plain glass bodies can be suspect.)
4. Does the glass fit the mount perfectly? (An ill-fitting body may be a replacement.)
5. Is the hinge on the lid undamaged?
6. If the handle is made from silver, is it in good condition?
7. If the handle is made from glass, is it free from chips and cracks?

174

Claret jugs

Silver-mounted glass claret jugs became fashionable in the middle of the 19thC, when they were produced in substantial numbers. The silver mounts were often highly elaborately decorated. They do not follow any set pattern of shapes and they were made in a wide variety of novel forms such as birds and monkeys. Silver-mounted decanters were also made but with the exception of grand Regency examples, they tend to be less sought after.

Glass bodies

The glass body of claret jugs was usually etched or engraved with

A naturalistic claret jug, maker's mark indistinct, London. 1863, 10.5in (26.5cm) high, 33.5oz, F

A novelty fox claret jug, by James Howden & Co. of Edinburgh. 1844–5, 11.75in (30cm) high, 54oz, C

some form of decoration and is often elaborately shaped. The body in the main picture shown opposite is embellished with stars and the base is cut with a star pattern. The condition of the glass is of fundamental importance to the value, since replacing broken glass may be impossible.

Decoration on the mounts which corresponds to that on the body is a reassuring indication that everything belongs together. Jugs that have coloured glass bodies are likely to be Continental. Large cartouches on either side of the jugs were invariably engraved with inscriptions or armorials and blank ones should be carefully examined for signs of any erasures.

Condition

Poor design can lead to damage to the handle as some of these jugs are very heavy when full.

175

Claret jugs

*A William IV claret jug, by
Edward Barnard & Sons of
London. 1836, 13.75in (35cm)
high, 44oz, E*

*An Irish presentation claret jug, maker 'PL'
of Dublin, the tall neck with lid and flower
finial, the body with engraved presentation
inscription. 1844, 12.25in (31cm) high, F*

*A claret jug, by Robert Hennell of London,
retailed by C. F. Hancock, embossed with
foliate panels and pastoral scenes, with
naturalistic vine-clasped handle. 1854,
12.5in (32cm) high, 38oz, E*

*A claret jug, in the form of a Greek askos,
by John Samuel Hunt, Hunt & Roskell of
London, inscribed 'William Henry Wills
from Charles Dickens'. 1859, 8in (20.5cm)
high, C*

A claret jug, by Turner Simpson of London, with leaf-capped bifurcated scroll handle, chased throughout with foliate rinceaux on a matted ground, the neck with oval cartouche. 1866, 14in (35.5cm) high, 32.25oz, E

An Irish 'Armada' claret jug, by 'JS' of Dublin, profusely decorated with chased floral decoration, applied cherubs and lion head. 1871, 15in (38cm) high, 45oz, E

A Victorian 'Cellini' pattern crested claret jug, by George Fox of London. 1874, 13.75in (35cm) high, F

A Liberty & Co. Art Nouveau claret jug, Birmingham marks. 1901, 15in (38cm) high, 24.5oz, E

Wine coolers

*A wine cooler, by William Pitts of London, with applied fruit and foliate
garlands and moulded foliage. 1803, 11in (28cm) high, 119oz, C*

1. Is the body fully marked?
2. Is the cooler complete with collar and liner?
3. Are the collar and liner part-marked?
4. Does it form one of a pair?
5. Are any decorative motifs elaborate?
6. Has the decoration remained undamaged?

Wine coolers

Although wine coolers were made from the early years of the 18thC, most date from the late 18thC and 19thC. Wine coolers were usually made in three parts – body, liner and collar – and were sold as pairs or

A presentation campana-form wine cooler, by J. E. Terrey & Co. of London, engraved with the coats of arms of the Island of Barbados and mottos of Samuel Maxwell Hinds. c1842, 13.75in (35cm) high, 180oz, B

in larger sets. Many Regency wine coolers were made in silver gilt, which protects the decoration.

Collecting

Wine coolers tend to be very expensive items as they are big and invariably contain a large amount

of silver. Elaborate designs and decoration are especially coveted.

Marks

The body should be fully marked, usually on the underside; the other pieces should be part-marked in one of two ways:

• With the lion passant, maker's mark, and duty mark (after 1794).
• With a full set of marks apart from the town mark.

By the mid-19thC the collar and liner were integrated into one piece as in this pair below, made by Russian Carl Tegelsten in 1849. They are embellished with lavish cast and applied decoration, which adds significantly to the weight and value.

A pair of mid-19thC Russian wine coolers, by Carl Tegelsten. 1849, 16.5in (42cm) high, A

Wine coolers

A pair of wine coolers, liners and rims, by Digby Scott & Benjamin Smith for Rundell, Bridge & Rundell of London, with scrolling grape vines and masks above engraved coats of arms. 1806, 12.25in (31cm) high, 220oz, A

A wine cooler, the body with grapeleaf and grape decoration, with armorial engraving, maker's mark mis-struck, with London hallmark. 1812–13, 11in (28cm) high, 44oz, E

An Irish wine cooler, by Jas. Fray of Dublin, with moulded leaf decoration, the silver liner with sculpted grapeleaf and grape decoration. 1824–5, 9in (23cm) high, 122oz, D

A George IV Irish wine cooler, by Edward Twycross of Dublin, of urn form with repoussé cartouches surmounted by eagles above a continuous band of foliate decoration, the handles chased with shells and foliage. 1825, 11in (28cm) high, E

A German Bruckmann & Söhne Rococo Revival wine cooler, with gilt interior, with the engraved coat of arms of the Princes of Liechtenstein. 1888, 7.5in (19cm) high, 30oz, E

A presentation wine cooler, by Howard & Co. of New York, the bulbous body with half-reeded decoration, with scroll and foliate framed inscribed cartouche. c1893, 11in (28cm) high, G

A German Art Nouveau wine cooler, decorated with irises, marked 'MR', 'KB', '875' and with a six-pronged star. c1900, 12.5in (32cm) high, 94oz, C

A wine cooler, by William Hutton & Sons Ltd of London. 1904, 6.5in (16.5cm) high, G

Wine coasters

A pair of wine coasters, by Robert Hennell II of London.
1788, 5in (12cm) diam, F

1. Is the wine coaster fully hallmarked on the rim on the base?
2. Is the border damaged or excessively worn? Has the wood remained in reasonable condition?
3. Is there any damage to the silver where it turns over the wooden base?
4. If there is a central boss: is it marked? (Preferable but not essential.)
5. Does it have a crest or coat of arms? (Only if it has a silver base.)

Wine coasters

Wine coasters were first made in c1760 when they had wooden bases and intricately pierced bodies, often incorporating a small medallion for a crest. Later in the 18thC the sides of coasters were made of sheet metal pierced with geometric motifs or festoons, or sometimes bright-cut engraving. The wooden bases were now centred with a silver boss to hold the crest. The boss should bear the lion passant mark, and possibly a maker's mark. Check that the crest is contemporary as any that have been added at a later date are undesirable. Among the most sumptuous coasters are those made in the Regency period with silver bases.

Coasters were designed to hold decanters rather than bottles. Early wine coasters tend to have slightly higher sides than later examples. These coasters opposite are typical.

A pair of wine coasters, by Waterhouse & Ryland of Birmingham. 1811, 5in (12.5cm) diam, F

Condition

The underneath of the bases are covered in green baize to prevent the coasters from scratching furniture.

Marks

Most coasters are marked on the plain lower rim that overlaps the wooden base. Very early coasters are marked in the piercing and the marks may be hard to find.

Collecting

Coasters are widely available but, because they can still be used, are still relatively expensive. They were always made in pairs or larger sets; single ones are undesirable and worth a quarter of the value of a pair. The most opulent Regency coasters were made from silver gilt and had heavy cast sides.

A set of four silver-gilt wine coasters, by Digby Scott & Benjamin Smith of London. 1804, 7in (18cm) diam, C

Wine coasters

A pair of wine coasters, by R. & S. Hennell of London, the slightly baluster borders with convex fluted borders, the everted rim with gadrooning and shell and acanthus details. 1811, 7in (18cm) diam, F

A large wine coaster, by Edward Farrell of London, with cast husk and scroll rim, the sides engraved with a coat of arms within an embossed, wrap-around scene. 1818, 6.75in (17cm) diam, F

A pair of wine coasters, by John Settle & Co. of Sheffield, heavily embossed with foliate scroll decoration, gadrooned and foliate borders. 1818, 2.5in (6.5cm) diam, F

A wine coaster, by Rebecca Emes & Edward Barnard I of London, with beaded border and engraved circular medallion inset into the turned wood base. 1825, 7in (18cm) diam, F

A wine coaster, by John Settle & Henry Williamson of Sheffield, with pierced and chased vines and branches. 1830, 6in (15.5cm) diam, G

A pair of Victorian wine coasters, by Henry Wilkinson & Co. of Sheffield, with chased fruiting vine on the everted rim. 1838, 7.5in (19cm) diam, F

One of a pair of Irish wine coasters, by James Moore of Dublin, embossed with a girl riding a goat, windmills, animals, cherubs and buildings. 1843, 6in (15.5cm) diam, F

A 1920s wine coaster, by Georg Jensen of Copenhagen, decorated with bunches of grapes, design no. 229. 5.5in (14cm) diam, E

Wine funnels

A wine funnel and stand, by William Bond of Dublin.
1792, 4in (10cm) long, 4oz, F

1. Are the bowl and spout marked by the same maker and in the same year?
2. Has the spout been trimmed?
3. Is there a sign of any repairs where the hook joins the body?
4. Is the body plain?
5. Is any crest original?
6. Is there any damage to the piercing in the strainer?

Wine funnels

Wine funnels were used to decant wine from the bottle for serving it at the table. Although they were made as early as 1700 they do not appear in quantity until c1770. Late 18thC examples were made in two parts – a bowl and funnel. The bowl is pierced to strain any sediment from the wine. Where the two pieces join there is sometimes a plain circular ring that slots inbetween. This would have had muslin tied to it for extra efficiency but it has not often survived.

A Scottish provincial wine funnel, by Charles Jamieson of Inverness. 1787–1819, 5.5in (14cm) long, 2.5oz, F

Many wine funnels originally had stands but very few are found complete with these today. Considering the elaborate decoration on almost everything else connected with the drink trade, it is surprising that funnels are so plain.

Marks

The bowl, spout and circular disc of wine funnels should all be marked. However, because the funnels were used so often the marks are often badly worn or even missing.

Alterations

The wine funnel in the main picture opposite is typical of those made from the end of the 18thC onwards, which had spouts that curved off to one side so that the wine would trickle down the side of the decanter. The necks of decanters gradually became narrower and in order to fit the funnel into the vessel the curved spouts were trimmed down. An untrimmed funnel is far more desirable than a trimmed one. This Dublin wine funnel by William Bond from 1792 has managed to retain its stand. The stand is slightly raised in the centre and was designed to catch the drips from the funnel. A good Irish funnel and stand is always a popular piece, but something of a rarity.

A wine funnel, by John & Joseph Angell, in a fitted case. 1832, 4in (10cm) long, 1oz, J

Wine funnels

A George III wine funnel, by Hester Bateman of London, with gadrooned border bowl with beaded decoration. 1788, 2oz, H

A George III provincial wine funnel, by Thomas Watson of Newcastle, of usual form with reeded border. c1790, 5in (12.5cm) long, G

An ogee wine funnel, by Peter & Ann Bateman of London, the strainer with a reeded rim. 1796, 4.25in (11cm) long, 2.5oz, H

A wine funnel, by Robert Gray & Sons of Glasgow, the wide, shallow bowl with simple pierced decoration, reeded rim and simple clip. c1800, 5.5in (14cm) long, 4.25oz, G

A part-fluted wine funnel, by Thomas Johnson of London, with gadrooned and moulded borders. 1810, 6in (15.5cm) long, 5oz, H

A wine funnel, by John Cowie of London, the bowl decorated with part-fluting and a band of reeding, initialled 'M'. c1814, 6.25in (16cm) long, 4.5oz, G

A wine funnel, by Richard Pearce & George Burrows of London, with a fluted campana-shaped bowl. 1828, 6in (15.5cm) long, 5oz, H

A Scottish wine funnel and drip stand, by J. McKay of Edinburgh. c1826, 5in (12.5cm) long, G

Wine labels

An openwork wine label, incised 'MOUNTAIN'. c1760, H

1. Is the decoration crisp?
2. Do details of the decoration show through to the back? (If so, it has been stamped.)
3. Is it cast? (And therefore more expensive.)
4. Is the title unaltered?
5. Are marks legible on the back?
6. Is the decoration complete?
7. Is it still on its silver chain?

Wine labels

Wine labels were introduced in c1740 as a way of identifying the new types of wine that were gradually filtering into common circulation. The labels were hung around the neck of the wine bottle from a silver chain and although it is not essential for these to be present, labels without the original chain will be less expensive. There is an almost infinite number of styles available and a corresponding variety of names, some of which are obscure today (such as 'Mountain' and 'Vidonia'). Labels made in the 1850s

A wine label, by William Cooper of London, incised 'HOCK'. 1846, 2.5in (6.5cm) wide, 1oz, G

Collecting

Wine labels bearing obscure names are far more collectable than those with a common name such as 'Madeira'. A premium is paid for a group of labels made by the same maker, but generally labels are collected individually. The rarer ones are bought by collectors and can form a fascinating history of the tastes of late 18thC and 19thC drinkers. The use of labels declined when bottles became properly labelled.

Types and styles

Earlier wine labels were purely functional and tend to have just a plain reeded border. At the beginning of the 19thC, labels in the shape of a vine leaf were made, and later in the century grapes and vines with a scroll supported by putti were popular.

A wine label, by I. W. Storey & W. Elliott of London, incised 'MADEIRA'. 1811, F

just have the initials, and by the 1860s very few labels were made at all. With the exception of Regency wine labels, which are cast, most are stamped.

Wine labels

An early George III escutcheon wine label, by Richard Redrick of London, with borders of chased fruiting vines. c1765, F

A George III scroll wine label, by Hester Bateman of London, with feather edging. c1770, G

A George III crescent wine label, by Susanna Barker of London, with feather edging. c1780, H

A George III wine label, by John Robins of London, with bright-cut border. 1792, F

*A George III Irish wine label,
by J. Teare of Dublin, of canted
oblong form with a moulded
border. c1800, G*

*A George III wine label, by Joseph Willmore
of Birmingham, decorated with putti,
grapevine and a Bacchus mask. 1814, 2.5in
(6.5cm) long, G*

*A George III plain oblong
wine label, maker's mark 'PG',
unascribed, probably Scottish.
c1815, G*

*A set of Irish George IV wine
labels, by John Teare Jarr of
Dublin, with chased decoration.
1820-5, F*

Miscellaneous silver

The earliest silver was often bought for display purposes, and as a ready source of money if needed. This system changed in the early 18thC with the rise to prominence of a large merchant class and the introduction of steam-powered rolling mills, which together increased the number of potential buyers and reduced manufacturing costs. The early 19thC invention of spinning metal over a chuck on a lathe further reduced mass-production costs and, coupled with stamping and the use of dies, this revolutionized silver production techniques. Grand pieces of display silver remained expensive, but otherwise there was a huge upsurge in the production of domestic silver at lower prices, and for those who could not afford silver, plated silver. From the 18thC there is a vast amount of small or unusual items made in silver. Frequently, such pieces have been produced in areas away from London, in, among other places, Birmingham, Leeds, Cork, Dublin and Scotland. A number of others were made on the Continent, particularly in Germany, where a number of parcel-gilt novelties were produced and then exported for sale. Many of these novelty items date from the Victorian period onwards, when production costs were far lower.

The type, size and variety of boxes made for tobacco, snuff, smelling salts and numerous

A William IV agate and silver vinaigrette, by Thomas Shaw of Birmingham. 1835, 2.5in (6.5cm) long, G.

other substances is so expansive that the collecting of boxes has formed a whole new collecting area. Irish silver has many similarities to English silver of the period. Even in the 18thC many pieces were chased, and this tradition continued into the 19thC. Some silver produced for the domestic market is larger than its English equivalent, perhaps because Irish families were usually far bigger. An Irish peculiarity is the dish ring, made from the middle of the 18thC onwards to hold hot dishes at the table. Harp-handled cups and butter dishes of the early 19thC are also typically Irish.

Civil and religious strife in Scotland caused much of its old silver to be destroyed, and as elsewhere in Britain little secular silver from Scotland has survived from before the Restoration in 1660. Even more so than in Ireland, there are numerous small towns where silver was marked. Quaiches, used for sharing whisky around a table, are obviously Scottish in origin, mainly made in Edinburgh.

A number of minor guilds in England produced silver until the Act of 1697 prevented them from hallmarking their own wares. Most of the silver that survives is spoons, an area in which there is much research. A small amount of domestic plate made in Leeds and Hull has also survived. The anchor town mark of Birmingham frequently appears on an array of boxes produced

A cow creamer, by George Fox of London. 1867, 6.25in (16cm) long, 6oz, E

in the 18thC onwards as the town produced small silver items in their thousands. The price of Apostle spoons depends on a combination of condition and date – 16thC examples are much more desirable than later ones and anything before the reign of Elizabeth I is very rare indeed.

Inkstands

A shaped oblong inkstand, by Henry Chawner of London.
1792, 11.5in (29cm) long, 19.75oz, G

1. Is it marked in a line underneath the tray?
2. Are all of the bottles and the bell also marked with the same mark?
3. Is there a dip in the tray to prevent the pen from rolling around?
4. Do the borders of the bottles and bells match the border on the inkstand?
5. Are the tops of the bottles part-marked?
6. Is any crest or coat of arms original?
7. Is there any evidence of damage to the piercing on the pounce pot?
8. Is the method of securing the bottles intact?

Inkstands

Early 17thC inkstands were rectangular and large, with hinged lids, but these were soon replaced by a stand with three or four bottles – one for ink, one for sand or 'pounce', one for sealing wafers, and a final one for cleaning shot (to clean the pen nib). By the 1740s the number of bottles

A rectangular inkstand, by Joseph Hardy of London. c1822, E

tended to be only two – for ink and sand – and there was now a bell in the middle so that the letter writer could call a servant to take the letter away. Pounce – powdered cuttlefish bone – was dusted over the ink instead of using blotting paper.

Marks

Early inkstands are marked in a line underneath the tray, with the bottles and bell fully marked and the tops part-marked.

All the separate parts should be marked, although it would be hard to mark the sealing wax holder without flattening it. From 1800 fragile items were exempt from being marked.

Beware

Because bells are desirable in their own right they were often separated from the rest of the inkstand and sold individually. Replacement bells on inkstands tend not to be marked. Any inkstand that has its original bell is much more desirable, but today is something of a rarity.

By the middle of the 18thC inkstands had two glass bottles for different coloured inks. Check that the bottles match and are the same size and that there is no damage – sometimes the tops rattle loosely because the collars are missing. Also check the piercing on the feet for damage.

An oval inkstand, by James Le Bass of Dublin. 1823, 11.75in (30cm) long, 29.75oz, F

Inkstands

A shaped oblong inkstand, by C. Reily & G. Storer of London, with two mounted cut-glass bottles and a central box and cover, the cover with conical snuffer. 1836, 13.25in (33.5cm) long, 35oz, F

A shaped oval inkstand, by 'HW' of London, with baluster taperstick flanked by cut-glass ink bottles. 1873, 11in (28cm) wide, 14oz, G

A navette-shaped inkstand, by Charles Boynton of London, the two cut-glass bottles with gadrooned borders, the stand with a gadrooned border and with flowers at the quarters. 1899, 11in (28cm) long, 8oz, G

A plain oblong desk inkstand, by Mappin & Webb of Sheffield, with two inkstand holders flanking a pen well, raised upon four claw-and-ball feet, with a pair of glass inkwells with silver mounts. 1903, 9in (23cm) wide, 22oz, H

An inkstand, by Charles Stuart Harris of London, with the two bottles with silver tops flanking a box with a miniature chamber taperstick as the cover. 1903, 9.5in (24cm) wide, 19oz, G

An inkstand, by Walker & Hall of Sheffield, with pierced three-quarter gallery back, fitted with two wells and a pen depression. 1913, 11in (28cm) long, G

A George V oval inkstand, by A. & J. Zimmerman, Birmingham. 1916, 8in (20.5cm) wide, J

An inkstand, by D. & J. Welby of London, the compartmentalized top opening to reveal an ebonized wood pen rest, glass inkwells and sand pot. 1925, 9.75in (25cm) wide, E

Cow creamers

*A cow creamer, by John Schuppe of London. 1757–8,
5.75in (14.5cm) long, 4oz, D*

1. Does the piece have a fly-hinged cover?
2. Does the tail form the handle?
3. Is it marked by the famous immigrant Dutch silversmith John Schuppe?
4. Does the date mark fall between 1755 and 1775?
5. Is the coat textured or smooth?
6. Is there added decoration to the back?
7. Are the feet stable?

Cow creamers

Cow creamers are of Dutch origin. They were produced in Holland for a very short period between 1755 and 1775 and are rare and collectable today. They were made almost exclusively by the Dutch silversmith John Schuppe, whose mark is hardly ever found on anything else. Most creamers stand on four feet but a few have been fitted with grassy bases. With these it is important to check the base has not been added at a later date to disguise unstable feet.

Cow creamers tend to vary little, although some have particularly attractive expressions. The example opposite has a textured coat; others may have smooth coats.

Some cow creamers were made in the 19thC by Charles and George Fox, who are known to have supplied silver to Lambert & Rawlings of Coventry Street, London, who sold copies of antiques and curios.

German cow creamers

Many German creamers were made at the beginning of the 20thC. These are significantly larger than English ones and were probably designed to hold milk rather than cream.

A cow creamer, by George Fox of London. 1865, 6.25in (16cm) long, 6oz, D

Damage

Check that the cow creamer's feet have not cracked and been repaired.

Check also for cracks at the tail.

Hot milk jugs

Hot milk jugs were made from the beginning of the 18thC when it was fashionable to have hot milk in drinks rather than cream.

Most hot milk jugs date from the 1720s. These are ovoid in shape and stand on three feet.

The earlier style, which is even rarer, is baluster in form and can sometimes also be octagonal.

A Continental cow creamer, with purity mark '925'. c1900, 11in (28cm) long, 27oz, F

Card cases

Most card cases were made in Birmingham. Used to hold visiting cards, they are larger than vinaigrettes – about 4in (10cm) – and are flat to fit inside a pocket. Decoration can be die-struck and similar to that on 'castle-top' vinaigrettes. This card case made in Birmingham in 1842, right, is one of the more decorative examples, with an elaborate border and a die-struck image of St Paul's Cathedral in the centre. Because the cases were constantly being taken out of a pocket high-relief decoration such as on this example is susceptible to wear.

A castle-top card case, by Nathaniel Mills of Birmingham, chased with a view of St Paul's Cathedral. 1842, 4in (10cm) high, F

A castle-top card case, by Joseph Wilmore of Birmingham, chased with a view of St Paul's Cathedral and St George's Chapel, Windsor. 1842, 4in (10cm) high, F

A castle-top card case, by Nathaniel Mills of Birmingham, with chased view of King's College, Cambridge. 1847, 4in (10cm) high, 2.25oz, F

A castle-top card case, by David Pettifer of Birmingham, embossed in relief with the Royal Exchange, London. 1848, 4in (10cm) high, 2oz, F

A castle-top card case, by Alfred Taylor of Birmingham, chased with a view of the Brighton Pavilion. 1854, 4in (10cm) high, D

A castle-top card case, by Hilliard & Thomason of Birmingham, embossed in relief with Westminster Abbey. 1868, 3.75in (9.5cm) high, 2oz, F

A castle-top card case, by George Carstairs of Edinburgh, engraved with a view of Calton Hill and the Royal High School. 1857, 3.75in (9.5cm) high, 2.5oz, E

Snuff boxes

Silver snuff boxes to hold ready-grated snuff were made from the second quarter of the 18thC onwards. A premium is paid for a box depicting a particularly sought-after pastime – for example, golfing scenes are extremely desirable.

Decoration is cast and chased and the value depends greatly on the condition. A box with worn details or where the pattern on the base has rubbed as a result of being pulled along a table will then of course be worth considerably less than one in good condition.

A 'squeeze-action' snuff box, maker's mark 'WF' crowned, the cover engraved with a squirrel. c1690, 2.5in (6.5cm) long, 0.5oz, F

A 'squeeze action' snuff box, by John Wilkins of London, engraved with a bird with foliate scroll decoration. c1699, 2.5in (6.5cm) long, 1oz, E

A silver triple-compartment snuff box, decorated with figures, the sides chased with fruit, flowers and shells. c1740, 2.75in (7cm) diam, 4oz, F

A double snuff box, by Phipps & Robinson of London, later engraved with a scene of the Mansion House. 1791, 3.25in (8cm) long, 3.5oz, D

A pocket snuff box, in the form of a fox head, maker's mark 'WP', London. 1792, 3.5in (9cm) long, 5.25oz, D

A silver-mounted ram's head table snuffmull, by Jonathon Millidge of Edinburgh, the horn with five tools suspended from chains. c1853, 17in (43cm) wide, D

A novelty snuff box, in the form of a jockey cap, by E. H. Stockwell of London, with gilt interior. 1878, 3in (7.5cm) long, 2oz, G

Vesta cases

Vesta boxes made to hold matches have become increasingly more collectable over recent years. Dating from c1880 onwards, they were made in a wide variety of shapes and sizes. Any unusual item of silver will command a premium.

Novelty pieces from the late 19thC show how any shape was used for vesta cases. The boar, dog and footballer's leg shown here, as well as golfing and bowling scenes, command high prices. Base metals were often used in an imaginative way to make less expensive items.

A novelty vesta case, maker's mark 'SB&S' of Birmingham, in the form of a footballer's leg kicking a ball. 1884, 2.5in (6.5cm) high, 0.5oz, G

A novelty vesta case, by Thomas Johnson of London, in the form of a boar, with button thumb press and spring-loaded cover. 1885, 2.75in (7cm) wide, 1.25oz, F

A vesta case, by Sampson Mordan & Co. of London, enamelled with a mounted lifeguard. 1890, 2.25in (5.5cm) long, 1oz, E

A vesta case, with maker's mark 'S.M.L.' of Birmingham, in the form of Mr Punch's dog Toby. c1890, 2.25in (5.5cm) high, G

A late 19thC silver and enamel vesta case, Gorham Mfg Co. of Providence, RI, decorated with a golfer lining up a putt. 2.25in (5.5cm) long, D

A Russian novelty vesta case and cigar cutter, by Theodor Nugren of St Petersburg, in the form of a jug. 1896–1908, 2.25in (5.5cm) high, F

A vesta case, maker's mark worn, Birmingham, decorated in low relief with figures playing bowls. 1907, 1.5in (4cm) diam, G

Vinaigrettes

Vinaigrettes were first made towards the end of the 18thC and continued to be produced until the middle of the 19thC. Designed to be carried in a pocket, they are much smaller than snuff boxes. Inside there is a pierced hinged silver grille, possibly still holding a piece of old sponge underneath, which would have originally been soaked in smelling salts. Earlier vinaigrettes are very simple with crudely pierced grilles, whereas later ones have elaborate piercing. The inside is always gilded – if not, the box has been altered or repaired. Most are rectangular, and many were made in the shape of purses. Vinaigrettes can be engraved, cast, chased or stamped with scenes of well-known private houses, cathedrals and monuments.

A vinaigrette, by Matthew Linwood of Birmingham, engraved with Lord Nelson, the grille stamped: 'The Victory' and 'Trafalgar, Oct 21 1805'. 1805, 1.25in (3cm) long, E

A vinaigrette, by John Wells of Birmingham, in the form of a reticulated fish, the head hinging to reveal gilt liner beneath. 1817, H

An engine-turned vinaigrette, by Isaac Rowley of London, with a micromosaic Dutch tulip collecting scene. 1821, 1.75in (4.5cm) long, D

A vinaigrette, by Mary Ann & Charles Reily of London, the cover inset with an enamelled lake scene, with engine-turned sides. 1828, 2.5in (6.5cm) long, D

A castle-top vinaigrette, by Nathaniel Mills of Birmingham, depicting St Paul's Cathedral. 1843, 1.75in (4.5cm) wide, E

A novelty vinaigrette, by H. W. Dee of London, in the form of a railwayman's lantern, with a revolving, three-colour lens. 1870, 1.25in (3cm) high, 1.5oz, F

A cornucopia vinaigrette, by Sampson Mordan & Co. of London, applied with die-stamped parcel-gilt and pierced work borders. 1873, 3.25in (8cm) long, G

Nutmeg graters

Made only in the late 17thC, these very small boxes – usually between 1in (2.5cm) and 2in (5cm) in diameter – have a hinged lid and base and a compartment to hold the whole nutmeg. Inside there is a grater grille. Usually the boxes are teardrop-shaped as in the example on p211 (bottom left) or they have a domed lid – to accommodate the oval-shaped spice. They are popular, and because they are relatively uncommon they tend to be relatively expensive. Check that the hinge is not loose and that the grille is undamaged.

A nutmeg grater, maker's mark 'JC', 'JE' or 'DE', the cover engraved with a rose, with pull-out tubular grater. c1690, 2.5in (6.5cm) long, 0.75oz, G

A nutmeg grater, maker's mark 'IA', with two internal compartments, a pull-off base and cover and a tubular grater. c1690, 3in (7.5cm) long, D

A heart-shaped nutmeg grater, by Thomas Kerr of Edinburgh, with twin hinged covers, decorated with geometric designs. c1700, 1.5in (4cm) long, 1.25oz, E

A nutmeg grater, by Thomas Phipps & Edward Robinson of London, in the form of a covered vase, hinged to reveal a blued steel grater. 1804, 2.75in (7cm) high, D

A nutmeg grater, by Robert Keay of Perth, engraved with a crest and motto, hinged base. c1820, 2in (5cm) long, 1.5oz, D

A mid-19thC Chinese nutmeg grater, teardrop-shaped with a hinged cover and base and signed with Chinese character marks. 1.75in (4.5cm) long, E

A novelty nutmeg grater, by Hilliard & Thomason of Birmingham, realistically modelled as a strawberry. 1859, 1in (2.5cm) long, 0.5oz, D

Pincushions

Pincushions only became a necessity once sewing implements were mass-produced during the middle of the 19thC. Like other decorative elements, pincushions gradually moved out of the upper-class boudoirs and into the parlours of the middle classes. They were crafted from bone, celluloid, wood, ivory, porcelain and very fashionable silver. Novelty cushions modelled after various animals with velvet pinning-fabric mounted on their backs became particularly popular in the early 20thC.

A pincushion, by Adie & Lovekin of Birmingham, in the shape of a standing bulldog. 1905. 2.5in (6.5cm) long, G

A pincushion, by Adie & Lovekin of Birmingham, shaped as a standing camel. 1906. 2.25in (5.5cm) long, H

A pincushion, by Collins & Cook, Birmingham, in the shape of a standing bull. 1906. 2.5in (6.5cm) long, G

A pincushion, by Boots Pure
Drug Co. Ltd. of Birmingham, in
the shape of a seated kangaroo.
1908, 1.75in (4.5cm) high, F

A pincushion, by Pithey & Co. of
Birmingham, modelled as a bear with
movable arms and legs. 1909, 1.5in (4cm)
high, F

A novelty pincushion, by Levi & Salaman
of Birmingham 1910, modelled as a robin
holding a golf club, standing on a hatpin
stand. 1910, 2.5in (9.5cm) high, G

A novelty pincushion, by Gorham Mfg Co.
of Providence, RI, in the form of a hare,
import mark Birmingham. c1927, 2.5in
(6.5cm) high, G

Caddy spoons

Caddy spoons were introduced when tea caddies no longer had a cap that could be used as a measure for the tea. They were made in vast quantities from the last quarter of the 18thC, mostly in Birmingham by the same smallworkers who made boxes and wine labels. They are made from sheet or die-cast silver.

Caddy spoons were produced in an infinite variety of designs, and any which are unusual or rare are particularly collectable, especially examples in the shape of a jockey cap or eagle's wing.

A filigree 'jockey cap' caddy spoon, unmarked, Birmingham, initialled 'H'. c1800, 2in (5cm) long, G

A rare 'eagle's wing' caddy spoon, by Joseph Wilmore of Birmingham, with textured plumage. 1832, 3in (7.5cm) long, F

A caddy spoon, by Charles Fox II of London, with a fluted and matted bowl and a shell terminal. 1838, 4in (10cm) long, F

A caddy spoon, by John S. Hunt of London, with a snail shell terminal and a scallop-shaped bowl. 1853, 2.75in (7cm) long, F

A caddy spoon, by Francis Higgins of London, the gilded, fluted bowl with a wavy edge border. 1853, 2.5in (6.5cm) long, H

A caddy spoon, by John Figg of London, with an openwork leafy stem and a fluted bowl. 1856, 4in (10cm) long, G

A caddy spoon, by Omar Ramsden of London, with a knotted tendril stem set with a crimson enamelled boss. 1919, 3.5in (9cm) long, E

Stirrup cups

Stirrup cups were used for drinking a toast at hunts, and by the nature of their shape they could not be put down until the vessel was empty. They were first made in the 1770s and continued to be produced

A pair of fox-mask stirrup cups, by Peter & Ann Bateman of London, the interiors silver-gilt. 1798, 5in (12.5cm) high, 12oz, C

throughout the 19thC. Most common stirrup cups are those in the shape of fox masks; others are in the shape of greyhounds. The earliest stirrup

A stirrup cup, maker's mark, 'CT' & 'GF', London, in the form of a boar's head. c1856, 4.75in (12cm) high, 18oz, E

cups tend to have longer noses and are more stylized than those from the reign of George IV, which are shorter and more textured.

Later stirrup cups can be cast, making them much heavier than late 18thC examples, which are normally raised or stamped.

With a few expensive exceptions stirrup cups were infrequently made in silver gilt.

An early 20thC stirrup cup, by Tiffany & Co. of New York, in the form of a stag's head, with gilt interior. 6in (15.5cm) high, 12oz, F

A stirrup cup that can be traced to an exact hunt is particularly desirable.

Marks

Stirrup cups were marked in a line around the neck and the marks are frequently difficult to discern within the decorative chasing.

Quaiches

Quaiches originated in Scotland and therefore are particularly popular with Scottish collectors. They were filled with whisky and passed around the table to share. They vary little in design and can be quite small – 4in (10cm) in diameter, including the handles – and solid.

Early quaiches, unmarked or with the maker's mark only, tend to be larger than later examples, which sometimes served as communion

A quaich, by Peter Aitchison of Edinburgh, the turned wooden bowl with silver mounts chased with a border of thistles. c1810–20, 4.5in (11.5cm) wide, F

A quaich, by Charles Fowler of Elgin, the lugs with wriggle-work border. c1809–24, 4.75in (12cm) wide, 2.25oz, D

cups in the way that beakers and occasionally tankards were in the United States. The handles are initialled rather than the body. The word derives from the Scottish Gaelic *cuach* meaning a cup. Traditionally, quaiches are made of wood. Quaiches began to be made in silver in the 1660s.

The origins can be traced to the Highlands and a romantic notion is that one of their ancestors was the scallop shell in which drams of whisky was served to welcome guests in the Highlands and Islands. Like shells, quaiches were wide and shallow. They became popular at the end of the 17thC in the main centres of Edinburgh and Glasgow. The shape has remained the same for 400 years.

The most collectable are those from rare provincial silversmiths.

An Arts and Crafts quaich, by Alwyn Carr of London, the handles cast with a Tudor rose, centred with a green-stained chalcedony cabochon. 1921, 8.25in (21cm) wide, F

Silver plate

Sheffield plate

Sheffield plate enabled the new merchant classes to buy items that closely resembled silver for a fraction of the cost. Consequently, many plated items are domestic wares such as entrée dishes and candlesticks. Plating was introduced in 1742 by Thomas Bolsover, a cutler from Sheffield. He is said to have accidentally discovered that melted silver could adhere to copper while repairing a knife in his workshop, and soon he was using the process. A silver sheet was placed onto a copper ingot, and all the air removed by hammering. Another layer of copper was applied to protect the silver and the 'sandwich' was then placed in a hot fire until the silver melted and fused to the ingot (silver melts before copper). If the ingots were then put through a rolling mill the metal could stretch to an almost infinite length without the silver leaving the copper. The process was soon used for larger items such as entrée dishes and

soup tureens. A good way to identify Sheffield plate is to run a fingernail underneath the edge. If there is a rim it is Sheffield plate. Sheffield plate was not made in any quantity until the 1770s. From the 1830s onwards it was also applied to a nickel silver base, popular because less silver was required to cover the base metal, which was white.

An Early Period Old Sheffield plate tea caddy. c1785, 5.25in (13cm) high, H

*A 19thC novelty
silver-plated
walrus decanter.
13.75in (35cm)
long, E.*

Close plating
Close plating was developed in c1779 for covering steel. The molten-hot metal was dipped into a mixture of liquid tin, covered with a paper-thin layer of silver foil, which was stamped onto the metal with a cloth-covered hammer, and then soldered. The technique was used particularly for knives, forks and spoons and other small items that were difficult to make from Sheffield plate. Candle snuffers are well-suited to close plating.

Electroplate
A far less expensive and quicker method of manufacture than Sheffield plating is electroplating. No fusion was required and all the handles, feet and finials that had previously needed to be made in two halves and filled with lead could now be cast in German or nickel silver and then plated in a vat. In little more than a decade the Sheffield plate trade had died out almost completely. It is useful to remember that whereas the surface of Sheffield plate used Sterling Standard, electroplate uses pure silver, which gives a whiter, harsher colour.

Electrotyping
Electrotyping enabled copies of complicated items to be produced easily. The technique was perfected by Elkington & Co. in the 1850s. They subsequently took on a Frenchman, L. Morel Ladeuil, to design pieces that they could profitably copy. The process involved the electro-deposition of metal in casts of an object, and then backing the casts with base metal. Accurate multiple copies of pieces could then be produced.

Sheffield plate

*An Early Period Old Sheffield plate cup, with the motto
'Mea Gloria Fides'. c1765, 7in (18cm) high, H*

1. Is it made from silver on copper?
2. Is there a silver shield?
3. If it is holloware, is there a seam up the back between the handle sockets?
4. Is there little if any copper visible through the silver?
5. If there is any decoration, is it flat chased?
6. Are any applied borders lead-infilled?

Sheffield plate

Sheffield plate was introduced in 1742, giving people the chance to buy silver-looking items at affordable prices. More novelty items were made in plate.

Condition

Condition is of utmost importance when you are buying Sheffield plate. If a piece is worn the copper will show. This is inevitable and although some copper can look attractive, the wear will only get worse, and pieces with large areas of copper showing should be avoided.

Check carefully for evidence of items being repaired with lead solder, as this will significantly lower the value.

Two Middle Period Old Sheffield plate tankards. 1785–90, 7.5in (19cm) high, H

Decoration

Any decoration on Sheffield plate is usually flat chased. If most Sheffield plate were to be engraved the incision would go right through to the copper, which is unsightly.

Some early plate will have a thicker layer of silver that is incorporated into the body so that the decoration could be engraved. In order to decorate a piece of Sheffield plate with a crest or coat of arms, a pure silver shield would be 'rubbed in' to the metal – the surface would be prepared and a silver rectangle or disc fused onto the body to bear the engraving.

Entrée dishes

Entrée dishes and their heater bases were often made in silver plate, and many silver examples had plated heater bases to keep the price down.

A Middle Period Old Sheffield plate coffee pot. c1790, 10in (25.5cm) high, J

Sheffield plate

*A pair of Old Sheffield plate candelabra, each
with central gadrooned urn finial issuing
two scrolled candle branches with trumpet
sconces. c1800, 14.5in (37cm) high, F*

*A pair of Old Sheffield plate sauce tureens,
of navette outline, the rim with gadrooned
details, raised scroll handle with acanthus
terminal. c1800, 8in (20.5cm) wide, G*

*A pair of Old Sheffield plate wine coolers,
by Matthew Boulton of Sheffield, of classic
campana form with egg-and-dart borders
and acanthus leaf decoration. c1810,
10.25in (26cm) high, D*

*A pair of early 19thC Old
Sheffield plate wine coasters,
of fluted form raised on a
barrow of rustic design.
19.25in (49cm) long, G*

A Late Period Old Sheffield plate soup tureen, with a gadrooned border and reeded handles with mask decoration. c1820, 13.5in (34cm) long, G

A Late Period Old Sheffield plate tea urn, with shell and scroll borders, a square base and on four paw feet. c1820, 17.5in (4.5cm) high, G

A pair of Late Period Old Sheffield plate candlesticks, profusely decorated with flowers, husks and scrolls. c1825–30, 10.5in (26.5cm) high, H

A pair of Late Period Old Sheffield plate wine coolers, in the Rococo Revival manner, the campana-shaped bodies engraved with armorials. c1830, 11in (28cm) high, F

223

Electroplate

*An electroplate wine cooler bucket, by Elkington & Co. of
Birmingham. c1860, 11.25in (28.5cm) high, F*

1. Is it fine quality?
2. Is the piece marked with the company's date or alphabet system
   and the maker's mark?
3. Does it have a PODR (Patent Office Design Number)
   (see p226)?
4. Is any gilding in good condition?
5. Is the plating also in good condition?

Electroplate

Sheffield plate virtually disappeared in the 1840s with the introduction of electroplate, a far more efficient and less expensive method of producing silver-looking goods. Although an electroplated goblet is recorded as early as 1814, it was not really until Elkington & Co. took out a patent for electroplating in 1840 that the process became widespread. The company soon had control of the market, buying out their competitors and employing the best craftsmen.

An electroplate candelabra garniture, by Elkington & Co. of Birmingham, the bases with coats of arms, the vine and leaf-wrapped scroll stem with putti. c1870, tallest 29.5in (75cm) high, C

A pair of electroplate wine coasters, by Elkington & Co. of Birmingham. c1870, 7in (18cm) diam, G

Method of manufacture

Electroplating involved putting a metal object in solution in a tank with a positive wire attached to a silver anode. A current was then passed from the positive to the negative. This resulted in a fine sheet of silver being applied to the object, which was whiter and harsher in appearance than Sheffield plate. Initially, the base metal was copper, but later nickel was used, hence the lettering EPNS (electroplated nickel silver), which is stamped on many electroplated wares.

Marks

Elkington & Co. developed their own system of marking. From 1841 and 1848 the company adopted the numbers 1 to 8 for the years, after which they used letters of the alphabet placed in different shields, beginning with the letter K in 1849, and starting the alphabet again in 1865, 1886 and 1912.

Electroplate

PODR

In 1842 the PODR system was
introduced to register designs
with the patent office.
The relevant number corresponds
to a date before which time the piece
should not have been made. The
number often appears on plate as
many novelty items were made in
plate rather than silver. Electroplate
items are less easily damaged than
Sheffield plate as the borders and feet
are no longer filled with lead.
If damaged, the pieces are very rarely
worth repairing.

*An electroplate centrepiece, by Elkington &
Co. of Birmingham, the rockwork base with
a stag beneath palm trees supporting a cut-
glass bowl. c1870–80, 20in (51cm) high, F*

*A silver-plate teapot with ebony handle,
designed by Christopher Dresser,
manufactured by James Dixon & Sons,
marked 'J.D. & S. 2274'. c1879, 9in (23cm)
wide, A+++*

*A late 19thC electroplate turnover
dish, by Martin, Hall & Co. of
Sheffield, on ram's mask and hoof
legs with foliate festoons. 12.75in
(32.5cm) wide, J*

*A late 19thC pair of electroplate
wine coolers, by Elkington & Co. of
Birmingham, of flared urn form, the
waist applied with fruiting vines.
11.5in (29cm) high, E*

*A Victorian novelty
electroplated spoon
warmer, modelled as a
shell mounted on a rocky
base. 6in (15.5cm) long, J*

*A late 19thC silver-plated wine cooler, by
Adams & Shaw of Providence, RI for Tiffany
& Co., with elaborate scrolled shell and
foliate borders, and floral and acanthus
decoration. 12in (30.5cm) high, F*

*An Art Nouveau silver-plated wine
cooler, by WMF of Geislingen,
decorated with raised foliate motifs
and a moulded mermaid and lizard.
c1900, 13in (33cm) high, E*

Index

Acknowledgements

Bearnes Hampton & Littlewood
St Edmund's Court,
Okehampton Street,
Exeter, Devon, EX4 1DU
www.bearnes.co.uk
p58tr, p91bl

Bellmans Auctioneers & Valuers
Newpound, Wisborough Green,
Billingshurst,
West Sussex, RH14 0AZ
www.bellmans.co.uk
p83tl

Bigwood Fine Art Auctioneers
Old School, Main Street,
Tiddington, Stratford-upon-
Avon, CV37 7AW
www.bigwoodauctioneers.com
p67tr

Bonhams
101 New Bond Street,
London, W1S 1SR
www.bonhams.com
p197l

Capes Dunn
The Auction Galleries,
38 Charles St, Manchester,
Lancashire, M1 7DB
www.capesdunn.com
p75tr, p91br, p139br, p147bl

Cheffins Fine Art
Clifton House, 1 & 2 Clifton
Road, Cambridge, CB1 7EA
www.cheffins.co.uk
p139tr, p199tl, p205tl

Decodame
853 Vanderbilt Beach Road,
PMB 8, Naples, FL
34108, USA
www.decodame.com/antiques
p71br

Dee Atkinson Harrison
The Exchange Saleroom,
Exchange Street,
Driffield, YO25 6LD
www.dee-atkinson-harrison.co.uk
p177br

Dorotheum
Dorotheergasse 17,
Vienna, Austria
www.dorotheum.com
*p14, p22bl, p23br, p32br, p33tl,
p51tr, p51br, p54bl, p55tl, p55tr,
p66tl, p94tr, p94bl, p94br, p95tr,
p105l, p115, p119tl, p122bl, p131tr,
p140br, p145br, p151bl, p151br,
p160tl, p180tr, p180bl, p181tl, p181bl,
p201l, p216cr, p227br*

**Dreweatts & Bloomsbury
Auctions**
Donnington Priory Salesrooms,
Donnington,
Newbury, RG14 2JE
www.dnfa.com/donnington
*p1, p10, p15, p22br, p31l, p39l,
p39r, p43br, p45l, p45r, p46br,
p47tr, p48, p50bl, p51tl, p52,
p57r, p59bl, p62tr, p63tr, p63bl,
p63br, p74tl, p75tl, p75bl, p82br,
p88, p94tl, p95br, p102tr, p106tr,
p107tl, p109r, p120, p125r, p126tl,
p127tr, p130tl, p130tr, p130bl,*

*p131bl, p143l, p144br, p146tr,
p146br, p147tl, p153l, p154tr, p162
p165bl, p167l, p168bl, p168br,
p188bl, p189tl, p196, p197r,
p198bl, p203tl, p203bl, p207tl,
p217br, p222bl, p223tr*

Dunbar Sloan
7 Maginnity Street,
Wellington, 6011
www.dunbarsloane.co.nz
p137l

Ewbank's
London Road, Send,
Woking, GU23 7LN
www.ewbankauctions.co.uk
p188tl

Fieldings Auctioneers
Mill Race Lane,
Stourbridge, DY8 1JN
www.fieldingsauctioneers.co.uk
p165br

Freeman's
1808 Chestnut Street,
Philadelphia, PA 19103, USA
www.freemansauction.com
*front cover, p21l, p25l, p25r, p32tl,
p32tr, p42tr, p42bl, p43tr, p54tl,
p55bl, p60, p61r, p63tl, p67bl,
p70tl, p70tr, p73l, p89r, p90tl,
p90tr, p90bl, p90br, p97l, p98tr,
p98bl, p99tl, p99bl, p99l, p99r,
p102tl, p102bl, p102br, p103bl,
p111bl, p113, p122br, p123tr,
p123br, p141bl, p149l, p150tl,
p151br, p152, p154br, p180br,
p199br, p216bl, p224, p227tl*

T W Gaze & Son
Diss Auction Rooms,
Roydon Road, Diss,
Norfolk, IP22 4LN
www.twgaze.co.uk
p23tr

Goodwins Silver
15 & 16 Queensferry Street,
Edinburgh, EH2 4QW
www.goodwinsantiques.com
p83br

Gorringes Auction House
15 North Street,
Lewes, BN7 2PD
www.gorringes.co.uk
p20, p78tl

Hartleys
Victoria Hall Salerooms,
Little Lane, Ilkley, LS29 8EA
www.andrewhartleyfinearts.
co.uk
*p91tr, p93l, p158, p163r, p198tr,
p198br*

James D. Julia Inc.
PO Box 830,
Fairfield, ME 04937, USA
www.jamesdjulia.com
p33bl

Auktionshaus Kaupp
Schloss Sulzburg,
Hauptstraße 62,
79295, Sulzburg, Germany
www.kaupp.de
p93r, p95bl

Law Fine Art
Ashmore Green, Ashmore
Green Road, Newbury,
Berkshire, RG189ER
p174

Lawrences
The Linen Yard,
South Street, Crewkerne,
Somerset, TA18 8AB
www.lawrences.co.uk
*p58bl, p83bl, p119tr, p137r, p142,
p155br, p164tr, p198tl, p204br,
p205br, p206bl, p209br, p210br,
p211bl, p226br*

Leslie Hindman Auctioneers
1338 West Lake Street,
Chicago, IL 60607, USA
www.lesliehindman.com
*p16, p29r, p43tr, p61l, p71bl,
p107bl, p155tl, p161tr*

Lockdales
52 Barrack Square,
Ipswich, Suffolk, IP5 3RF
www.lockdales.com
p123bl

Lyon & Turnbull Ltd.
33 Broughton Place,
Edinburgh,
Midlothian, EH1 3RR
www.lyonandturnbull.com
*p7, p9b, p12, p13l, p17, p18, p23tl,
p24, p27l, p31r, p33tr, p37, p38,
p40, p42br, p44, p53l, p54tr, p56,
p64, p68, p69l, p71tl, p82tl, p83tr,
p86, p92, p97r, p103tl, p103tr,
p105r, p106bl, p106br, p109l,
p110tr, p121r, p129l, p134, p136,
p138tr, p143r, p144tr, p145bl,
p147tr, p150br, p154tl, p160bl,
p161br, p164tl, p165tl, p169bl,
p175l, p175r, p176tr, p176bl,
p177tr, p179l, p179r, p184tl,
p187l, p188br, p195, p200, p201r,
p203br, p205bl, p206tr, p207tr,
p209tr, p217l, p219, p222tl,
p222tr, p222br, p223br, p226bl*

Matthew Barton Antiques
25 Blythe Rd, London, W14 0PD
www.matthewbartonltd.com
*p13r, p53r, p106tl, p128, p133,
p138br, p140bl, p146bl, p149r,
p173, p176tl*

Justin Neales
3 Evesham St, Alcester,
Warwickshire, B49 5DS
www.jneales.com
p46tr, p58br, p144bl

Northeast Auctions
93 Pleasant St,
Portsmouth, NH 03801
www.northeastauctions.com
p111tr

Olivia et Emmanuel
85 Rue des Rosiers,
93400,
Saint-Ouen, France
www.oliviasilver.com
p55br

Pook & Pook
463 East Lancaster Avenue,
Downington, PA 19335, USA
www.pookandpook.com
*p30, p36, p43bl, p58tl, p66tr,
p89l, p110bl, p110br, p122tl,
p123tl, p126bl, p135, p138tl,
p139bl, p140tr, p145tl, p163l,
p184br*

Quittenbaum
Hohenstaufenstraße 1,
D-80801, Munich, Germany
www.quittenbaum.de
p141tl, p155bl

Rago Arts
333 North Main Street,
Lambertville, NJ 08530, USA
www.ragoarts.com
p181tr

Ritchies
21 Dundas Square,
Unit 1101, Toronto,
Ontario, M5B 1B7,
Canada
www.ritchies.com
p59tl, p59tr, p107tr

Roseberys Auctions
74-76 Knight's Hill,
West Norwood,
London, SE27 OJD
www.roseberys.co.uk
p62tl, p208bl, p208br

Silver Fund
330 Worth Avenue, Palm Beach,
FL, 33480, USA
www.thesilverfund.com
p67br, p185br

Skinner Inc.
The Heritage on the Garden,
63 Park Plaza, Boston,
MA 02116, USA
www.skinnerinc.com
*p54br, p55tl, p66bl, p103br, p131tl,
p140tl, p155tr, p178*

Sloanes & Kenyon
7034 Wisconsin Avenue,
Chevy Chase, MA,
20815, USA
www.sloansandkenyon.com
p98br

Sotheby's
34/35 New Bond Street,
London, W1A 2AA
www.sothebys.com
*p21r, p46bl, p96, p98tl, p180tl,
p225r*

Sworders Fine Art Auctioneers
14 Cambridge Road,
Stansted Mountfitchet,
Essex, CM24 8BZ
www.sworder.co.uk
*p46tl, p49l, p125l, p157l, p159l,
p186, p188tr*

Tennants Auctioneers
The Auction Centre,
Leyburn, DL8 5SG
www.tennants.co.uk
*p22tl, p23bl, p28, p41r, p66br,
p69r, p70br, p71tr, p75br, p91tl,
p146tl, p150bl, p153r, p154bl,
p164br, p169br, p171, p177tl,
p177bl, p182, p185tl, p185tr, p194,
p202tr, p202bl, p202br, p203tr,
p208tr, p217tr, p225l, p226tr*

Toovey's
Spring Gardens, Washington
West Sussex, RH20 3BS
www.tooveys.com
p129r, p176br, p199tr, p213br

Tring Market Auctions
Brook Street, Tring,
Hertfordshire, HP23 5EF
www.tringmarketauctions.co.uk
p199bl

Van den Bosch
58 Davies St,
London, W1K 5JF
www.vandenbosch.co.uk
*p27r, p30 br, p87, p131br, p151bl,
p156r*

Adam A. Weschler & Son, Inc.
909 E Street, NW, Washington,
D. C. 20004, USA
www.weschlers.com
p70bl, p138br

Wiener Kunst Auktion
Palais Kinsky Freyung 4,
A-1010, Vienna, Austria
www.imkinsky.com/de
p99bl

Woolley & Wallis
51/61 Castle Street,
Salisbury, Wiltshire, SP1 3SU
www.woolleyandwallis.co.uk
*back cover, p3, p6, p8t, p8b, p11,
p19l, p19r, p22tr, p29l, p32bl, p41l,
p42tl, p47tl, p47br, p49r, p50tl,
p50tr, p50br, p51bl, p57l, p59br,
p62br, p65l, p65r, p72, p73r, p74tr,
p74bl, p76, p77l, p77r, p78tr, p78bl,
p78br, p79tl, p79tr, p79bl, p79tr,
p80, p81l, p81r, p82tr, p82bl, p85,
p95tl, p99tr, p100, p104, p106bl,
p107br, p108, p110tl, p111tl, p111br,
p114, p116, p117l, p117r, p118tl,
p118tr, p118bl, p118br, p119bl,
p119br, p121l, p122tr, p124, p126tr,
p126br, p127tl, p127bl, p130br,
p139tl, p141tr, p141br, p144tl, p148,
p150tr, p156, p159r, p160tr, p160br,
p161tl, p161bl, p164bl, p165tr, p166,
p167r, p168tl, p168tr, p169tl, p169tr,
p172, p183l, p183r, p184tr, p184bl,
p185bl, p187r, p189tr, p189bl,
p190, p191l, p191r, p192tl, p192tr,
p192bl, p192br, p193tl, p193tr,
p193bl, p193br, p204tr, p204bl,
p205tl, p206br, p207bl, p207br,
p209tl, p210tr, p210bl, p211tl,
p211tr, p211br, p212tr, p212bl,
p212br, p213tl, p213tr, p213bl,
p214tr, p214bl, p214br, p215tl,
p215tr, p215bl, p215br, p216tl,
p218, p220, p221l, p221r, p223bl,
p223bl, p227tr*